BLACK WIDOW

BLACK WIDOW

A Sad-Funny Journey Through Grief for
People Who Normally Avoid Books with
Words Like "Journey" in the Title

LESLIE GRAY STREETER

Little, Brown and Company

New York   Boston   London

Little, Brown and Company
Hachette Book Group
1290 Avenue of the Americas, New York, NY 10104
littlebrown.com

First Edition: March 2020

Little, Brown and Company is a division of Hachette Book Group, Inc. The Little, Brown name and logo are trademarks of Hachette Book Group, Inc.

The publisher is not responsible for websites (or their content) that are not owned by the publisher.

The Hachette Speakers Bureau provides a wide range of authors for speaking events. To find out more, go to hachettespeakersbureau.com or call (866) 376-6591.

ISBN 978-0-316-49071-9
LCCN 2019949820

10 9 8 7 6 5 4 3 2 1

LSC-C

Printed in the United States of America

For Brooks and Scotty

We got something snappy.

—Guy Patterson, That Thing You Do!

Contents

BLACK WIDOW

I

Now, This Is a Story All About How My Life Got Flipped— Turned Upside Down

Here," says the nice enough salesman, pointing to the lawn crypt to his right, "your loved one would go in first, with his head facing this way. And when it's time, you would go in headfirst, so your heads and hearts are touching for eternity."

Umm...thanks?

Nice Enough Salesman makes reference to concepts like eternity and togetherness and how, forty or fifty years from now, the body that used to be me can be placed facing what's left of what used to be my husband, Scott.

All I can hear is *Your husband is dead. Your husband is dead. Pick a box, your husband is dead.*

You'll forgive me for not thinking clearly right now, because my husband very recently dropped dead in front of me while we were making out. And when I say "very recently," I mean yesterday.

I have to pull myself together and deal with this sometime—well, right now, probably—but what I really want to do is jump on the golf cart from which my mother is nervously watching me and drive us to the nearest bar.

I should be at the *Palm Beach Post,* the newspaper I write for, finishing a column about the free drinks Scott and I were supposed to have had as "research" for a cocktail story. That "research" was supposed to have happened yesterday afternoon, right around the time our stunned, sobbing relatives began landing at the airport. We were supposed to be celebrating the job Scott was supposed to start on Monday before we picked up our adorably goofy baby boy from day care.

Supposed to doesn't mean crap.

Instead, I'm at a cemetery trying to pretend that any scenario that involves my husband in a crypt is at all okay. Having to even think about this crypt instead of free drinks is pissing me off.

"I guess it's not legal to keep him in a refrigerated

travel-trailer in my backyard?" I ask Nice Enough Salesman, who looks startled. *The widow's got jokes!* Perhaps this is not the time?

"Unfortunately, no."

I feel like we're doing some twisted vaudeville bit—he's an appliance salesman with a baggy suit and a comically large flower on his lapel trying to talk a dizzy housewife into buying a newfangled washing machine, but she has to wait for her husband's permission to buy it. The joke—and this is a good one—is that she can't ask him 'cause, you know...he's dead.

That isn't funny at all, is it?

I cannot fully fathom how we got here, because for the past twenty-four hours I swear I keep blacking out and somehow materializing in jacked-up places like funeral homes and cemeteries. I do know this: My Scotty, who had not been feeling well for a few days, got up in the middle of the night to pee. He noted that our almost-two-year-old son, Brooks, was still sleeping soundly across the hall and asked if I wanted to make out. Since I still had a few hours before the deadline for a story I was writing, and because I don't turn down twilight make-outs, I agreed. Then we started kissing until he stopped me—he never stopped me—and said that something was wrong.

I turned on the light and saw Scott's head shaking, kind of like a blender that keeps rumbling three seconds after you turn it off. I wasn't really awake yet, so I couldn't quite understand what was happening, what I could not stop from happening. I can't tell you how much time passed—thirty seconds or a hundred years—but as quickly as Scott had started shaking, he stopped moving.

"What's happening?" I half screamed, half pleaded. Scott didn't answer. All I know is that finally he let out two desperate, involuntary breaths.

Then he didn't breathe again.

That was yesterday.

So what I want is for Nice Enough Salesman to give me a minute, because things are kind of fucked up right now. I'm planning a traditional-ish Jewish funeral for my husband when I'm supposed to be planning his forty-fifth birthday party. I'm black and Baptist, and he's a white Jewish guy. I feel a little out of my depth. Also, what the hell? We are in the middle of finalizing the adoption of the aforementioned sleeping baby, who's been with us since he was six months old but is still not yet legally ours. I actually just got back from Maryland, the state of all of our births, after one in a series of very stressful legal proceedings to make sure we get to keep him. I'm supposed to be focusing on that, not standing here in this stupid cemetery deciding whether Scott's body will spend eternity in a fancy wall or in a hole in the ground in the Jewish section or in some nondenominational section so he can be buried with me, his black Baptist wife. My understanding is that I can't be buried in the Jewish section when I eventually die. I can't imagine that's going to be any time soon, but then again, Scott's not supposed to be dead either. So I don't know what to tell you.

As Nice Enough Salesman continues his sales pitch, I look back over at my mother, who sits several yards away on a golf cart with my twin sister, Lynne, my best friend, Melanie, and Scott's cousin Kim, whom the black Baptists have brought along for her specific area of expertise.

"We need a Jewish person," I told her that morning when she showed up at our house, in shock but wanting to be useful. When someone you love dies, that's what you do. You do everything you can to be useful so you don't have time to remember that someone you love has just died.

My sister and Melanie, both of whom came in from Baltimore yesterday and are running on fumes and stunned adrenaline, are eating out of a bag of chips. I think Mel got them on the plane. Wait, am I hungry? Probably. To date, my mourning diet has consisted of wine, cake, and last night's garlicky hummus, which I probably still smell like. Not my problem. I have lost a pound. And, yes, even tragic and disorienting sudden death cannot stop me from weighing myself. I guess I cried off a pound. Is it wrong to be happy about that?

"Thank you for telling me about the crypt," I say, turning back to the salesman, who seems to have finally finished his pitch, even though the crypt seems super-creepy and there's no way in hell we're doing that corpse head-to-head thing. "I know you haven't mentioned it yet," I continue because I seem to be expected to keep talking, "but how much do your mausoleums run?"

I can see Cousin Kim shaking her head. She's pretty sure that Scott wouldn't have wanted a mausoleum, but since he insists on being dead and I have to be here anyway, like I'm car shopping, I might as well check out this part of the showroom.

"We don't talk about numbers here. We like to keep that for the end," Nice Enough Salesman says. "Don't want to overwhelm and confuse you."

Too late, man!

In the past forty-eight hours, my life—the one that included a husband and baby and job and was generally awesome—has become a great sparkly clusterfuck. I haven't even figured out how to tell my not-quite-two-year-old that Daddy's not actually working late. I have not the first effing clue how to even process this toxic cloud that's blown up my life. But I'm pretty sure I can handle a price list.

Nice Enough Salesman is very pleasant, so I smile and get back on the cart. He drives it to a small fenced-in area of grave markers of various shapes and sizes inscribed with an eclectic collection of names—a Korean here, an Irishman over there in the corner, some random WASPs.

"Some Random WASPs. That's a good band name," I whisper to Scott, who cannot hear me.

I remember once interviewing a man whose wife had been killed in a hit-and-run maybe six hours before he answered the phone and found an apologetic young reporter on the other end asking him about losing the love of his life. I told him repeatedly how sorry I was, but he stopped me.

"No," the newly minted widower insisted, "I want people to know who she was, that she wasn't just some name in an accident report. And if I wait too long, the shock will have worn off, and I won't be able to do this anymore." I thought I understood then, when I was single and twenty-four, but now at forty-four, I think that man was a wizard.

I don't know how he formed words and coherent thoughts in that state, but he's my hero. Somebody's gotta do this shit, and since I don't have staff or a personal secretary, it's me. And I better do it now before reality sets in and the shock gives way to despair and inertia and I just can't do anything anymore.

So I get off the cart and grab the bag of chips. It's probably tacky to be surveying the tranquil garden where my true love will be residing forever while wiping artificial barbecue dust off my fingers. It'll have to do. Nice Enough Salesman beckons me farther in, explaining that there are available plots in this section. It's the United Nations of Dead Folks, and therefore depressingly perfect, because Scott and I were an old-person Benetton ad.

Next to the space Scott might be moving into is a large shiny headstone displaying the smiling face of a young black kid. I guess he is maybe fifteen? *Was* fifteen. Shit. I can't bear it. I look away.

"Hey. Stop dropping chips on the dead people," my mother hisses from the golf cart. She is also a widow, having lost my daddy to the rudest, dumbest kidney cancer imaginable three years ago. And yes, I'm a forty-four-year-old woman who still calls her parents Mommy and Daddy because we're tangentially Southern and that's a thing.

Mommy, as an unfortunate expert in this stuff, knows that dropping chips on the manicured lawn of Benetton Grave Village is not a thing I should be doing. But I'm a tragic widow now, so I do what I want.

A minute or so later, we head back to the funeral home to make some decisions, because apparently some have to be made, and I seem to be where the sad, shitty buck stops.

"What do you think?" my mom whispers.

"I think we're going to go with the garden," I say. See? I'm making decisions! Getting shit done! Why, just yesterday, about six hours after I returned home from the hospital without my husband, I picked out Scott's casket, with help from Kim and my two other guest Jews, Scott's cousin Kenny and my friend Shana. I wonder if I'm being insensitive, asking these people I care about to tap into their lifelong knowledge of Jewish customs and explain everything to me. How would I feel if one of them was married to a black person and summoned me to Ebenezer Whatever Baptist-AME Church as the spokes-Negro?

I think I'd understand.

Anyway, yesterday we'd picked out the casket—a traditional austere plain pine box and finalized other stupid funeral details, and I knew that this was only the first toe-dip into an Olympic-size pool of horrible that I was going to have to eventually swim all the way through. I didn't even want to get into that pool. But I have no choice but to wade in, sit there, and smile as some guy walked me through sales packages—*effing packages*, like we were picking spa services.

So, as distasteful as it is, here we are today, deciding that Scott will be buried in Benetton Village next to a nice black teenager and, one day, me. He will be in that lovely, Jewish-law-compliant pine box. There will be punch and finger foods and a montage of photos, some taken just three or four days ago on the beach with our still-clueless boy when we used to be happy and Scott used to be alive.

I liked that life.

I want it back.

But that seems to be the only package they don't offer here.

2

Love Is All Around

Not long after Scott died, I told his best friend Jason, whom he'd known since they were kids and who was hurting just as bad as I was, that I wanted to write a book about this hellish thing we'd been plunged into. He paused for a moment, so long a moment that I was afraid he was going to tell me it was a bad idea.

"I think you should," Jason finally said, the volume in his voice rising just so, "but don't just make him some guy that died. Don't just write about him dying. *Write about Scott.*"

So, ladies and gents—meet my husband. Wish he were here to read along with you. I hope he would have dug it.

As I told you a little while back, Scott was Jewish and white, and I am Christian and black. None of that gave us a moment's hesitation when we got together; there was no movie montage of us in our separate apartments staring into the distance going, "How will I ever bridge these differences? What's it all for? Why am I hearing sad violins and mournful eighties jazz saxophones?"

I'd like to say that we were drawn to each other's pure natures and generosity, but we also shared a love of soap operas, Cheetos, and barely concealed giggling about inappropriate things in delicate public situations. We once found ourselves at a mightily fancy Palm Beach dinner party that I was writing about, something right out of a Marx Brothers movie I would not have been cast in. We were seated at different tables, because I guess that's what fancy people do. There we were, this random pauper couple sitting next to strangers, noticing that the only other black people in attendance were clearing the dishes. We tried to be chill about it, but it's not like we didn't already stand out.

Scott told me later that one of the ladies at his table was going on and on about a trip she'd taken to the Ivory Coast to shoot white doves, and all he could think was *You went to Africa to kill the Jewish bird of peace.* We cracked each other up, me and that guy.

There were so many fish-out-of-water situations that became the kind of stupid-funny memories the two of you giggle about as you fall asleep at night, your toes touching in the dark and your sleepy love thoughts making it funnier than it probably was. Consider my introduction to kugel at his cousin's Yom Kippur break-fast. I was holding up the line trying to figure out what all these noodle-looking dishes were when I really just needed to move the hell on because folks had been fasting and were getting testy. "It's all just kugel!" one of his exasperated aunts finally shouted. *"Pick a kugel and go!"*

My dating life had been…interdenominational, but I had always thought that eventually I'd marry a Christian guy, because that's what I was supposed to do. My family thought I would too.

"So, I understand that he's a Jew," my grandfather the Reverend Lester James Sr. said when he called to congratulate me on my engagement to some dude I'd been dating just six months and whom he hadn't yet met.

"Yes, sir."

"I don't suppose he's a black Jew?"

"No, sir. Just a regular white one."

Sigh, followed by a long silence. Then: "Well, they do have black Jews, you know. Just saying."

By the time my granddaddy died, two years later, he and Scott were tight, having bonded over all the things they had in common, like their shared love of reading and movies and hearing themselves talk. Also, they both loved me. That was a small victory, because my mom's side of the family, of which my granddaddy was the patriarch, is very protective and kind of proper in an austere, churchy-suit sort of way. Like the Obamas but with less cash.

My granddaddy had worked very hard to get us as far in life as he could; he and his then-young family, including my mom, literally had to flee South Carolina when his own father was murdered in the 1950s by a white policeman who thought he was uppity. That and the general experience of being a black man growing up during Jim Crow made him understandably wary of some situations. He was mostly cool with most people until they gave him reason not to be, but I don't think he ever considered the possibility that he might one day have a white grandson-in-law. And since he was a preacher, he *really* wasn't expecting the Jewish part.

By the time Scott and I got together, I'd had plenty of crushes on men of all nations. What they all seemed to have in common was being wrong for me, because it turns out that I have horrific taste in men.

When my extended family met Scott—who was an upgrade in every way—I hadn't brought around a boyfriend in ten years, and the last one they'd met was also Jewish and white. So it wasn't exactly an M. Night Shyamalan movie twist—Bruce Willis is dead and Leslie's dating a Jew! Because they're well-mannered, proper people, my family was immediately hospitable. Maybe they realized that love is love. Or maybe they really wanted grandbabies. I was in my late thirties, and we'd had to buy plane tickets to come meet everyone, and they knew I wouldn't shell out cash money on some fool I wasn't serious about. All of us were on our best behavior, on both sides of the table. If Scott had said something dumb, I know it would have been reported back to me later. In detail.

But everybody liked him, because Scott was really hard not to like. He went out of his way for people—he was always the guy who jumped up and refilled everybody's drink. I knew he'd won over my granddaddy for sure by the time of my sister's wedding, a month after Scott's mom had died. (So much dying.) My granddaddy had lost his mom, too, so they had that in common. And they talked, walking and nodding quietly. Both such good talkers. Also, Scott and I were already married by then, and no foolishness had been reported back to my granddaddy, so he happily

17

accepted that this unexpected but nice not-black Jew wasn't going anywhere, though sometimes he got mixed up and called him Stu.

"It's *Scott*," I would hiss under my breath, but my husband always shushed me. "He likes me," he'd say. "Stu's close enough. Let it go." (He occasionally called my brother-in-law A.C. "A.J." so neither of them took it personally.)

Granddaddy and Scott's finest moment was one Father's Day when my husband automatically stationed himself next to my stepgrandmother Bernie, who was frail and ill at the time. Scott patiently and lovingly helped her lift her water glass to her lips, gently wiped her mouth, whispered to her which dish was which, and made sure she got the next helping of whatever she wanted. I got up to thank him for being so attentive, but he waved me off.

"She reminds me of my *bubbe*," he explained. A man who loves his *bubbe* is a good man. If my whole family wasn't already in love with him, they were sold later in the meal when Scott volunteered to call Red Lobster about getting our massive and expensive takeout order very wrong.

"I'm Jewish and negotiating is my thing," he said, smiling, and my family, well versed as we are in the art of the Strongly Worded Letter, were amused enough to let him try, politically incorrect stereotypes notwithstanding.

18

By the end of the phone call he was explaining in a raised Al Pacino tone of voice that not only was our order wrong, but the tartar sauce was expired.

"We have elderly people here! My wife's *grandmother* is sick! You want her to eat *expired tartar sauce?*" Over the top? Sure. Effective? You know it! Red Lobster did not, it turns out, want my elderly stepgrandmother to consume expired seafood condiments, so they refunded more than half of the meal to my aunt's credit card. By the time Scott hung up, he was the family hero.

"Stu! Stu! Stu!" they chanted in celebration, because we are all tacky and think we're clever. This confused my dad, who was just coming in at the time and had missed the whole thing.

"Why is everybody calling Scott 'Jew'?" he asked.

By then, it seemed like Scott and I had known each other forever. Technically, we almost had, if *knowing each other* means "I used to sit behind you in Humanities class and know everyone you know but not quite you." Scott and I actually met in high school in Baltimore in 1985, although we barely spoke to each other back then. He'd gone to college with my twin sister, and I'd kept vague track of him in that "How's that dude we went to high school with?" sort of way.

If you're only hip to the very white John Waters retro version of Baltimore or the crime-laden *The Wire* version, here's a thing you should know: it's a very ethnic city, specifically a very black one, or at least it was when I was growing up.

Dig: I had a black pediatrician, a black dentist, and black teachers. I also knew the black men who clung to their paper-bag-wrapped bottles in front of the liquor store down the street from my house, which was also a few blocks away from Morgan State University, the historically black college where my parents started dating.

My experience is *a* black experience, not *the* black experience. *The* black experience is not a thing. Some of the unenlightened might describe twerking and pimping and *Good Times*–like stuff as "black." Those things are, indeed, a part of black culture. But when I and most of the people I grew up with describe things as "super-black," we're talking about highly educated people with dreads or Afros who protest everything and call each other "my sista" or "my queen" and who got arrested for demonstrating against apartheid in the 1980s and '90s. *Black Panther* is super-black. Harvard's Professor Skip Gates and the mannered, casual way he calls celebrities "my brotha" is super-black. *What's Happening!!* was as black to me as *The Cosby Show,* which was the closest thing I had to watching myself on TV growing up. Given what we now know about Bill Cosby, that seems unsettling, but it wasn't in 1984. I'm not a wizard.

There are myriad ways of being black, just like there are myriad ways of being white, Latinx, Native, Asian, and anything else one identifies with. I'm not sure why this is still so hard for people to get. Scott grew up in Baltimore at the same time I did, so our personal experiences were both similar and foreign to each other. His neighborhood was historically Jewish, but by the time he came around, it was somewhat black-speckled. That gave him an advantage that most white people do not have, in that the whole spectrum of blackness was not a mystery to him. (Some might not think that's an advantage, but screw those people.) He had black teachers, black bosses, a black Little League coach. He also got mugged by a black guy who tried to jack his leather coat at the bus stop on his first day of high school; Scott lied and said it was really pleather. (The guy let him keep it.)

Scott was more into some things considered culturally black than I was. For instance, while I was headed to Lilith Fair and sobbing along to Jewel songs, he was a classic-hip-hop fan who worshipped KRS-One and NWA. But he never claimed to be black, or blacker than me. I have deleted people on Match.com who claim that shit. If your profile says that you think quoting Snoop Dogg or having always had a crush on Janet Jackson is equivalent to being black, then you can go sit down somewhere.

Scott understood that and understood parts of my culture while passionately embracing his, because he was smart enough to recognize where the boundaries were fluid and where there was ebb and flow. He felt deeply Jewish, more than he felt just white, even though he also acknowledged that he carried the privilege of being white and would be seen as such where I...would not. He was also white enough that sometimes restaurant hostesses assumed we weren't together even when we were literally holding hands and had been sitting next to each other in the lobby for fifteen minutes.

As much credit as we gave ourselves for being aware and appreciative of each other's cultures, that shit became *real* real when we married into them. I remember going to his cousin's house not long after our wedding, already self-conscious about being the only non-Jewish and black family member. (And, yes, as my granddaddy said, there are many black Jewish people. I just am not one of them.) There was a Hasidic rabbi there who had straight-up told Scott not to marry me because I wasn't Jewish. I felt like the heroine in some overwrought 1980s movie of the week called *The Color of Love* or *The Price of Love* or some clichéd thing with *Love* in it.

When the rabbi and his family rolled in, I decided to be the bigger person and offer him my hand, which he declined. I was about to get all "We Shall Overcome" about it until Scott reminded me that Hasidic men can't touch women they aren't married to, and I felt kinda stupid. I'd been two seconds from causing a scene and looking hella ignorant. Whoops.

Our respective faiths were huge to us, both religiously and culturally. Over time, I came to understand what being Jewish meant to Scott, and he came to understand more about what being black and Baptist meant to me. We learned these things because we loved each other enough to learn. Note, young people—anyone who doesn't love you enough to do that doesn't love you.

Scott was raised by Reform Jewish parents but had an Orthodox grandfather, so he was very into social justice and also read Hebrew really well. He had been through eleven-three years of Hebrew school and said he used to go to hours-long Orthodox services where you couldn't leave, eat, drink, or see any girls. (He was one of the only people I ever met who found your typical black Baptist church service, which is so long you wish you'd packed a lunch, breezy and short.)

By the time he was an adult, Scott wasn't attending services regularly, but he was still passionate about being Jewish because of the strength and endurance that it taught him and also because a religion with such a tradition of surviving oppression seemed sort of badass to him. "The holidays are basically 'They tried to kill us, and now we just eat,'" he explained. "Sometimes we fast before we eat. But there's always the eating."

I, however, was a hippie sort of black Baptist who, when we met, attended a mostly white nondenominational church that was generally a little more conservative than I dug but basically friendly. Scott loved me for my beliefs—he loved that I believed, period. Believing is hard when you're a grown-up, particularly when you move away from your sometimes cloistered community of like-minded believers and find so much new stuff to consider. Like, what are they doing over there? Let's look!

I admit that my faith is not the same as it used to be, that my questions are more…question-y. This is going to upset some of y'all, but I do not believe that my husband, who was Jewish and thought that Jesus Christ was a nice, rabble-rousing Jewish prophet with some good points but

who was not the Messiah, is in hell while some slave own-
ers who professed their belief in Christianity as they were
raping my ancestors are chilling with the saints. Miss me
with that foolishness.

But I still believe in God and in miracles and in the
divine, and so did Scott. We got that about each other. We
got each other. And I'd waited a long time for someone to
get me, because I can be a lot.

Ice-T once said that he and his former *Law & Order: SVU*
costar Richard Belzer got along so well because "he's Jewish,
I'm black, and the Klan's after us both." Scott and I joked
that if we'd heard it sooner, that line would have been in our
New York Times wedding announcement. His mom would
have been so pissed. But it would have been worth it.

Another part of my faith that Scott became acquainted
with, whether he liked it or not, was the not-sleeping-with-
him-before-marriage part. Yes, friends, by the time I recon-
nected with Scott in my late thirties, I was still holding out.
Technically. I'll give you a moment to be shocked.

You good?

Even at thirty-whatever, I still believed that I should not
have sexual intercourse, even though I admit my definition
of "sexual" became more strictly technical as time went on.
I kept changing the rules until the dudes didn't know what

the line was, because honestly I didn't either. I felt like there was some sort of inner buzzer in my head and also in my bra that would go off when I felt fingers going for the clasp. *Buzz!* That's all, man! No bra unclasping for you!

Waiting wasn't just for religious reasons at that point. By the time Scott and I found each other again, I'd waited so long that the idea of just jumping the next idiot who seemed at all interested felt like cheating. Not just on Jesus, but on myself. And I was very committed to not cheating on Jesus.

Just like my folks weren't surprised that the guy I married turned out to be a white dude, his parents weren't really shocked that he married a black girl, although he told me his mother would have liked it if I were a black Jew. He had dated black women before, and Latina women, and white girls who were not Jewish. This is not to say that if the perfect Jewish girl had come along, they wouldn't have been pleased. But they got me instead. They were cool with it.

Scott's parents were very open-minded in that well-read liberal way, both of them educators with master's degrees and a diverse group of friends. Sam, his dad, is a writer; he did PR for the public schools and taught at various colleges for years. I think he probably legit has some tweed jackets with patches on the elbows. His mother, Sharon, taught special ed and was always exquisitely dressed and went to the beauty salon every week, both for the beauty and the scene. When it came to her family, she was "ride-or-die" before that was a thing. I was very nervous about meeting her because by then Scott and I were serious, and I wondered if my being black would be a problem. He'd promised it wouldn't be, but Sharon, after all, was a Jewish woman married to a Jewish man raising Jewish children, and that's what she knew. But my mother-in-law also loved her son, and she loved me because she knew I loved him too. We all loved each other. Sometimes that's what love is—just getting each other.

I really got him.

I really miss him.

I think I already said that.

3

Believe It or Not, It's Just Me

Do you know what an origin story is? In comics and in the zillion-dollar film series based on them, it's the detailed journey of how a normal-seeming person winds up flying and shit. There are usually tights involved, and although I, too, have an origin story, it is blissfully tights-free.

I like to think of myself as a typical American girl, which sounds like either a kick-ass Tom Petty song or an over-priced historical doll. Again, I am neither of those things, but I do have something in common with the doll: we each come with an emotionally satisfying backstory and more than a few jaunty hats.

Also like me, those dolls start off as typical lasses who encounter some massive life-changing thing, like the Great Depression or war or, in the case of Addy, the first black American Girl, being born into slavery. That always seemed like a misstep, like if you're introducing black history to kids, perhaps you should start with a triumphant, non-bondage place in history. Where's that Shirley Chisholm for President doll?

Unlike Addy, my world-quaking event—widowhood—came in adulthood. I'd had ample time to figure out who I was before that particular life explosion. Before that moment, I guess my life was normal, although *normal* is relative, depending on who you are and where and how you grew up. As a black woman living in America, I've known my whole life that to mainstream America, my experience is not the norm. I am the other.

I'm not complaining. I love being black and would never wish otherwise because that's who I am. But it can be a challenge. To be a black woman in this country is never to have the illusion that you are the standard or that things in the wider culture were intended for you. If you've ever been told that you can't walk into the walk-in salon in the mall because the only stylist who knows how to do your hair is off today, you learn that real quick. It's not that they don't like you. They just don't expect you to be there because they're not thinking about your black ass. They probably forgot you existed until you showed up with your hair needing to be done and they're like, *Oh, snap! Black people! Why didn't anybody warn me?*

So much of my story might be considered all-American if not for my high melanin level. I was raised in Baltimore by churchgoing, well-educated, and happily married parents who bought their first house right down the street from their college. That didn't make us better than anyone else. But it just shows we were meeting criteria that still didn't always guarantee us consideration. They saved and struggled and traveled the world; they put their daughters through school and helped pay for their weddings and their own first houses. They taught us good, wholesome values. We watched Westerns and played softball, and I sang in several church choirs. And not only was I a Girl Scout, but my sister and I were even assistant Girl Scout leaders, at twenty-three, just because we wanted to be good role models and help shape the minds of young independent women.

We were saints, basically.

Even in my lovesick, self-pitying, bad-poetry-writing phase in high school, I knew that I was privileged and lucky. Not rich, but solid, with people who loved me. My family is a particular kind of bougie, not in the way that I see that term used on Twitter now, but in the age-old black-community way that describes either the very fancy or those trying really hard to look like they are. Sometimes it's an insult, like you're pretentious, but I claim that shit. We *are* bougie. That doesn't mean that we won't throw down if necessary and go off or at least ask to see your manager in a commanding tone if we feel disrespected. We ain't playing.

It has taken crappy things, like Scott dying, to remind me that I'm descended from badasses, scrappers, and little old ladies who will bless you out when you deserve it. In front of your mama. Members of my family endured riding in the luggage car on train trips south because of their skin color, survived the racially motivated murders of their fathers by police officers, and lived mostly happy lives punctuated by discrimination, death, and some frankly hideous shit. But they remained classy. You were on the porch holding a foil-covered paper plate of lemon cake as the door shut behind you before you realized how close you'd come to being thrown out by your wig.

My mother, Tina, finished her master's degree in social work while Lynne and I were in day care; she graduated the spring before we started kindergarten. My daddy, Ed, whom family and close friends called Butch, worked mostly in transportation, eventually as the operations manager for district school-bus services around the country. When I was a kid, I wished he did something cooler, like run Disney World. But as I got older, I began to understand that dependability and making a contribution to society were cooler than being able to cut the line at the next roller coaster. And school buses are the key to education for kids who might have no other way to get to school. They also paid for my prom dress, college, the down payment on my first home, and my Palm Beach wedding suite. School buses are everything.

Growing up, I always thought I was more like my daddy than my mother. We could both be singularly focused, sometimes efficiently, sometimes like impatient jackasses. We also shared an addiction to *Law & Order* and Patrick Swayze movies in which he kicked the hell out of everybody. (I personally enjoyed that he did all this ass-kicking shirtless.) We even once skipped church to watch *Road House*. ("Heathens," my mom said as she left to go pray for our souls.)

Lynne—my twin and my only sibling—and I are similar, but not in the way that other people always wanted us to be. We fit none of your popular twin stereotypes, which is to say we're not psychic, we weren't separated at birth like in *The Parent Trap,* and we're not in porn. So the intricacies of our twinness confused casual bystanders, so they took any minuscule difference between us and magnified it so they could tell us apart. My sister and I are both very nice people, but Lynne is nicer, so she became the Nice One and I became the Mean One. And if there was any perceptible weight difference between the two of us, the heavier one was the Fat Twin—some stupid woman at church once told me how great it was that I'd gained weight because now she could tell us apart. Yes! I'm risking diabetes just for you!

We were the only twins in our neighborhood and the only identicals in our grade, so everyone called us the Twins or, individually, Twin, something I stopped answering to in my twenties. You have a fifty-fifty shot of getting my name right.

Our neighborhood, Northwood, was mostly black, at least by the time we got there. It was really nice and not in the hood; more hood-adjacent. You could see the hood a couple of blocks away by the public library right next to the Chinese carry-out with the bulletproof glass. Just in case we thought we were too fancy.

My neighborhood always felt normal to me, and it wasn't until I started making friends from way outside of it that I realized that it might seem less-than to some, which made me defensive and angry. I was dropped off at home once by the mother of a white friend who lived in what would be considered a more upscale area because it had bigger houses, more trees, and, let's be honest, more white people. When she slowed down in front of my relatively small but neat home, smack-dab in the middle of a row of other neat homes, all of them with neat lawns, well-cared-for cars parked out front, she said, "This is *nice,*" clearly surprised at how not shitty and actually decent this urban black community was. I didn't say anything; I just got out of the car and felt weird about it. Apparently for decades! (Don't ever let other people make you doubt how cool you are. Don't ever give anyone that power.)

We moved into that house when Lynne and I were four and stayed until we were eleven years old and our family moved for a year and a half to Saudi Arabia because my dad was working with an American company contracted to create and run the public bus system. We got there in the middle of sixth grade and left at the end of seventh, which meant we had to go to eighth grade back in Baltimore at a completely different school a year before leaving that school and starting all over in high school. At the time, I was mad at my folks—especially in the really lonely moments—for foisting this on us, particularly in middle school, since the one thing all middle-school kids have in common around the world is that middle-school kids all suck.

As a parent now, I understand that my mother and father wanted us all to be together and were proud to expose us to new cultures, new places that most of my friends had never heard of. Before my sister and I left Baltimore, the kids in our class wrote us goodbye letters wishing us luck in Cairo or "Iraq/Iran," because what the hell did sixth-graders know about Middle East geography?

Our life in Saudi Arabia made me curious about life outside my own door, about people who were not like me, who believed things that I didn't. (It was also a place that didn't, at least at that time, sell Old Bay Seasoning, so my father, a man of faith and specific seasoning needs, smuggled a big-ass can into the Kingdom along with his cross and Bible.)

Lynne and I had always been well liked, albeit slightly weird and awkward—twins in bifocals who were once dubbed Eight Eyes because there were two of us. But when we found ourselves the only black kids in seventh grade in our American school in Saudi, we were suddenly pretty popular, like all those new kids in the books and movies I loved whose differentness made them remarkable. (We were the black, girl-twin Brenda and Brandon Walsh, a decade earlier and with Jheri Curls.) My weird was working for me for once.

Sadly, popularity could not protect me that year from being called "nigger" for the first time, by a kid who harassed me in class every day until he pressed a stapler into the back of my hand and pushed, the metal bracket just piercing my skin. They put him in a different class for physically attacking me, which didn't seem enough of a punishment to me, but we went to the only American school for hundreds of miles, so I guess there wasn't much more they could do to him. I guess.

Growing up not long after the civil rights movement, reciting the black-history buzzwords about slavery and lunch counters and MLK, I was aware that racism existed. But Saudi Arabia taught me personally what my place in the world might look like outside of my neat little corner of hood-adjacent Baltimore. People weren't always going to be happy to see me, and even those who were would sometimes have unrealistic expectations, like that I'd be a good dancer because I had the same original skin color and hair as early-1980s Michael Jackson. Maybe that's when I became a writer for real—I had to start cobbling together my own narrative and figure out what the theme was, no matter where I was.

We returned to Baltimore right before Lynne and I started eighth grade, and we moved right back into our same little house, which now looked smaller to me somehow. I had grown, and the house had stayed the same size. Everyone around me seemed to have stayed the same too. But in a year and a half I had seen the whole world, or a big damn chunk of it. I'd climbed a date tree in the middle of an oasis in the middle of the Saudi desert. I'd spent Christmas break in Madrid, marveled at paintings of unbelievably beautiful ladies in the Prado, and sung along to *The Best Little Whorehouse in Texas* with Burt Reynolds and Dolly Parton dubbed in Spanish, which our parents let us watch because we couldn't follow the specifics of the whorehouse thing. I'd eaten lobster on a plane, been yelled at by Bedouin for wearing short sleeves while playing baseball on my mostly male Little League team, and bought a *Grease 2* soundtrack CD in a case that had been helpfully edited by Saudi censors so that Michelle Pfeiffer's face was covered with black marker, an impromptu veil. For modesty.

I had lived a great adventure, breathed the air of the whole world, and coming back to the same few blocks of Baltimore was like trying to shove a hot-air balloon into a juice box. I wanted to tell my old friends all about what

I'd seen and done, but I didn't have the words. I felt *odd*. (I probably was.) But I so wanted to fit in again, as much as I ever had. Some of those old friends cut me loose. It was incredibly painful, but I got it. And one of the good things about being forcibly cut out of your old life is that you have no real choice but to find yourself a new one.

Middle school is a nightmare anyway, but there's a particular head-trip in having been popular and cool for a season in a faraway land and then returning home to find you're a dork again. If I still had all the hand-scrawled poems I produced at that time about feeling particularly poignant and special in my aloneness, I wouldn't show them to you because they were awful. But, again, they were the building blocks of a writing career. *Special aloneness* nearly made my résumé as a skill.

I was mostly dateless as a teenager, but that's probably a blessing, because I'm sure if I had dated more, I would have been so annoying and in my head, I'd have screwed it up. Also, I wasn't putting out. My church was morally conservative when it came to sex, modesty, and the necessity of wearing pantyhose in the sanctuary, but it was somewhat politically liberal in that we were a black church and thus down with civil disobedience, protests, and the Democratic Party. I was in middle school before I realized that in mainstream (read: white), Reagan-era society, all Christians were assumed to be Republicans. It was shocking! I was a fan of the radical Jesus the Bible actually described, the wild-haired, truth-telling, rabble-rousing, masses-feeding, widow- and disreputable-woman-defending rebel who would toss your superior, moralistic, money-changing ass out of the Temple and tell you about yourself. *That's* my guy.

I might have enjoyed free-flowing Hippie Jesus, but the hippie thing didn't extend to every aspect of my Christianity; I fully embraced the part of my religious upbringing that considered saving oneself for marriage a given. There were various random guys in high school I found cute, including this one white Jewish dude who thought he was a Beastie Boy who I barely knew but who I would be seeing again in a significant way in about twenty years. But those crushes were mostly unrequited. It would have been nice to have had someone want me enough to test my resolve, chasteness-wise. Hard to feel superior in a vacuum.

I did manage to have at least one legit boyfriend as a teenager, the too-hot-for-me son of one of my mother's coworkers. He was my first kiss—I remember him trying to slip his tongue into my mouth, and I shrank back like he'd tried to shove in jumper cables. It felt strange, and too much, and also too good, and—*Shut up, Leslie!*

The way that this whole holding-out thing was supposed to work was that you only dated Christian guys who were supposed to be committed to waiting too. But if we're being real, and I try to be, I'd have gone out with almost anyone who'd asked and who I thought was cute, because self-esteem and I needed to have a chat. Desperation isn't sexy, and the good Christian boys weren't interested, so it didn't much matter. I did date-dabble outside the church in college and in my early twenties, and I finally found guys who did want to test that resolve I was so smug about. Finally I got to be desired and not just a loser no one wanted to bone. I would usually say up-front, pre-make-out, that I was happy to kiss and all but that I would not be having sex with them. You will be absolutely not shocked to learn that this was usually the last time I made out with any of these people.

See, I thought to myself, *if this guy is not willing to consider waiting, then he's not the guy for me! It's self-selection.* Did I worry that I was going to self-select myself into cat-lady-hood? Of course. I think that fear affected my taste in men, which is to say again that I sometimes had very, very bad taste in men. For all of my supposed discernment and wisdom about not sleeping with anyone before I got married, I lowered, adjusted, or just shoved a big old stick of dynamite into my standards if it looked like someone was interested in me. *Did I say I needed you to have a good job? Well, you have a job, right? Some sort of job? Like, something you get paid for? Like, your mom gives you gas money? Okay! And yes, I did say I wanted to date only a very serious Christian like myself, but you go to church, right? Well, you've been to a church? Once? To use the bathroom? Well, God brought you to that church for some divine reason, and He blessed you, and you're blessed, and now, yes, please keep kissing me.*

Just know you're gonna have to stop...at some point. I'll say when.

Eventually I parlayed my questionable track record in men-choosing and historically unjustifiable optimism into a career: I became a newspaper columnist, telling stories not only of my community but of myself, from my 1990s Ethan Hawke obsession and love of hair bands to the heart of this amazing and sometimes messed-up country of ours. When I got to the *Palm Beach Post* in the early 2000s, *Sex and the City* was still a huge deal. After I worked my single girl-friends and our dating shenanigans into a few columns, my editor, Larry, suggested a column idea. We called it That Girl, in which I explored the county's eating and drinking and fun-type offerings in my signature breezy and slightly oversharing manner.

"It's like '*No* Sex and the City,'" he quipped, referring to the fact that the *Post* was a family publication and my stories about a new martini bar should not end with me taking home dudes from that martini bar. He didn't realize just how accurate his little joke was.

So because America is a magical place, awkward in-her-head Leslie became Black Carrie Bradshaw, except that I was much more sensible about shoes and bills, never made my married lover's wife chase me through their home in an attempt to avoid being caught, and was generally a better person, because Carrie was kind of the worst.

Also, I wasn't going to be single that much longer.

4

Love, Exciting and New!

 W hen did you know you wanted to marry me?"

I knew what Scott would say, but I always asked when I was having a needy moment and required validation. Everyone wants to be compelling enough to be fallen in love with at first sight, and I'm no exception.

"I knew the moment you walked into the bar," he'd always say, and sometimes at this point in Emotional Gimme Theater, he would kiss me on the nose in the way he knew I loved. That was his sweet story, and he was sticking to it. We hadn't seen each other since our senior year at Baltimore City College High School, but when our class was planning our twentieth reunion on Facebook, we realized we had lived a half an hour from each other in South Florida. He'd moved back to Baltimore by then but was planning to come down temporarily, so we agreed to get a drink. When Scott glimpsed me across a crowded bar for the first time since we were pimply children, he instantly knew I was his destiny. Or so he said.

"I thought you were the most beautiful woman I had ever seen, and I knew you were going to be my wife!" he'd insist. He was emphatic about it. The word *wife* is not sexy to everyone; to some it's probably a cold, cold shower. But coming out of Scott's mouth in his slightly nasal Baltimore accent, it made me want to pull the car over and do something wifely. It's such a *permanent* word. To me, permanency with the right person is irresistible. It might be scary when you're young, when the world laid out in front of you is so promising, it's like a Monopoly board full of properties waiting to be bought and you're standing at Go between the thimble and the top hat.

But it's different when you're older, when you've done enough of this dance to admit you can't always remember the steps so you just keep step-touching in place like a fool. You've lived a life. You have owned houses, built and ruined and rebuilt credit. You have constructed a career and a reputation that you're not too keen to let just any moron blow up. Plus, you're tired. Tired of assholes on Match.com who are obviously twenty years older than their pictures or who search for you on your first date but skip over you with their eyes a few times, unconsciously hoping that you're not actually who they're looking for. That shit *burns*.

I'd come to understand that a smart woman did not give *permanent* away to just any idiot who wandered into her life like he was hopping boxcars with all of his shit wrapped in a kerchief hanging off a stick. But Scott got it. We'd both made historically dumb choices in the romance department. I'd had my share of duds, and he had spent years before me with a woman who made him propose and then dumped him because her mother said she had to marry a doctor. I never met her but I'd like to shake her for hurting my baby and then hug her, because her dumbness gave me a husband. Scott and I had both fixed our sights on people who did not really want us, and we probably knew that they didn't want us long before the situation either died on its own or somebody straight-up murdered it.

We were different together. That first time we re-met, during a too-warm South Florida winter, the energy was…better than I thought, but also a little nervous. It occurred to me that maybe this wasn't just a friendly reunion between old friends who had never quite been friends but an actual *thing*. I didn't think it was a thing for me, at least not yet. I mean, this was *Scott Zervitz*, the same Scott Zervitz who used to sit in front of me in my ninth-grade Humanities class wearing an Audi hood ornament on a chain around his neck. (It was the 1980s.) I can still see his dark hair coming to a curly point at the base of his neck over the collar of some loud-patterned shirt that clashed with itself. He conducted between classes what he'd one day refer to in our *New York Times* wedding announcement as "a hallway business." He was a lot.

When we finished our crab soup and beer, he walked me to the valet stand and hugged me goodbye, then mentioned again that he was planning to be in town for a month or so, working in a relative's business. And even though I wasn't really interested, I remember thinking, *Okay, a month. I hope he calls me again.*

Meeting again after two decades was cute, but it's even cuter when you realize that we had been doing an unwitting dance around each other for years. I find myself imagining a lot of useless what-ifs, like what if Scott and I could've gotten over ourselves in high school and started dating then? And if not then, what about when he and my sister went to the same tiny little college? She used to mention him every once in a while because he was the life of whatever party he deigned to enter. I probably shrugged and then went back to talking about Kevin Costner movies or whether anyone could tell my purse was a knockoff.

"Do you remember me from parties at St. Mary's when I would visit Lynne?" I asked him once or twice. "Did you ever see me there?"

"No," he'd said. "If I had, I'd have asked you out."

"You never asked me out in high school," I'd groused. "And if you noticed me, why didn't you ask me out back then?"

I never really believed that Scott had liked me in high school. But about three years after he died, I chatted online with one of his high-school running buddies, and the friend confessed that he'd always wondered why Scott and I hadn't dated in high school because Scott had always liked me.

He always said he did but I never believed him, I typed.

Well, it's true, Scott's friend typed back. *Did you ever wonder why nobody ever pushed up on you in high school?*

Did he mean, did I wonder why I was sad and dateless and trapped in a futile single existence when everyone else seemed to be living in a John Hughes movie? Why, yes! It had crossed my mind!

That's because they all knew Scott liked you.

Plot twist!

Why didn't he ever say anything? I typed back, wondering if I needed to start blaming Scott for the more pathetic parts of my adolescence before remembering that this would now be useless.

I always assumed he had, Friend typed back.

Too bad I can't ask Scott about it, I replied. And it is.

As much as I tell myself that everything is as it's supposed to be, sometimes I still engage in pointless grief-drenched self-flagellation. It's like, if I pore over every detail of our lives together like they do in the movies, I'll discover some mystical glitch or wrinkle that can be unwrinkled, and I can just change it.

Please change it.

Please don't let Scott be dead. Don't let it be true. It happened so fast, you know? Just like that, so easy, like a shrug. If Scott's life—our life—could end with that little effort from the universe, like an afterthought, why can't the universe just shrug in the other direction and give him back to me?

I know, I know. It won't. Just a thing I think about.

After Scott and I started hanging out in Florida in our older, probably wiser incarnations, I kept telling myself that we were just friends. A few weeks after our first drink, I even flew to Vegas with friends and made out with some twenty-something British dude in a club under a hail of comped drinks, which are the most delicious drinks of all. I told Scott all about that later, when we were in love, admitting that I retroactively felt like I'd been cheating on him because although we were not dating when I made out with that guy, a small part of me sensed that he was in love with me. Kinda.

"That doesn't bother me," he said. "You were just killing time until you fell in love with me."

Man, Scott was cocky. It was sort of hot. And despite my insistence that this was platonic, my girlfriends thought otherwise. "You're spending a lot of time with that Z guy," my friend Vivian pointed out.

"Just a friend thing," I said, although Vivian, a veteran observer of my sometimes goofy dude-related judgment, raised her eyebrows at me like she knew something I didn't. I couldn't see it happening, but he was getting to me.

The day Scott finally asked me out for real, a less determined man would have thrown up his hands and given up, because it started with me blowing him off. We were supposed to see *Taken,* the Liam Neeson movie, at a theater in Boca about twenty-five minutes from my place. But I got caught up in a Cuba Gooding Jr. movie on TNT about Ben Carson. Yes, that Ben Carson. This may seem odd after Carson became a sleepy, ill-spoken member of Trump's cabinet, but for kids like us raised in Baltimore near Johns Hopkins Hospital, where he worked, he was a big deal. Staying home to watch the end made me late for the movie and was incredibly rude, but I kind of thought Scott would get it.

"Of course I get it," he said when I called him to sheepishly beg forgiveness for being late and asked him to wait for me so we could see the next show. "I'll wait."

I found out later that Scott had already seen *Taken*—twice—so his waiting around wasn't about the movie but about *me*. Ooh. He waited for this rude woman who had blown him off for a Ben Carson biopic, *then* asked if I had time that evening to have dinner. Intriguing...but I was supposed to head back to West Palm Beach and pick up my friend Stephanie at the airport. Still, I think I sensed that this dinner was the beginning of something more, something deeper, so I violated Girl Code and asked her roommate Lauren to pick her up instead.

Yes, I blew off a friend for a dude. But don't feel bad for Stephanie. She got home okay. And my friend Scott took me out to dinner at a nice seafood place and then asked if

I'd like to go out soon for what he termed our first official "date-date."

"Sure!" I said. "When?"

"Saturday," he answered.

If there's one thing that both the chronically single person and the veteran features writer in me knew, it's when all holidays fall, and that Saturday was Valentine's Day.

"Oh, no, let's do another night," I protested, explaining that such a commercially and emotionally loaded day put too much pressure on a first date, and wasn't there another less significant day we could go, and hey, aren't you listening to me?

He wasn't. He was certain. And so I agreed to go on my first date-date with Scott Zervitz on a day that I usually spent with girlfriends pretending that was just as cool. We actually already had plans for the night before Valentine's; I was reviewing a Natalie Cole concert at a fancy hall. I hadn't considered that date-date-like earlier, but now it seemed like too romantic an outing to go on the day before what was supposed to be the possible beginning of our romance. So I asked him to pick one or the other.

"Nope," he said. "I really want to see Natalie Cole, and I have something special planned for Saturday."

Pushy bastard. I liked it.

That Friday, I met him for dinner at the upscale outdoor shopping area that was around the corner from the fancy hall, and I remember watching his mouth as he ate hummus and garlic bread and thinking, *That's a lot of garlic. Am I going to kiss him? Do I want to kiss him?*

I think I wanted to kiss him. What the hell?

I should probably add here that the more I thought about the possibility of things working out with Scott, who was employed, educated, and not a sketchy person living in a boxcar, the more I knew I'd have to eventually tell him about the current state of my sex-having, or not-sex-having. I'd been in a semi-significant and retrospectively ridiculous long-distance relationship that had ended about a year before. The man involved had been cool with my convictions in the beginning, when he thought that maybe he was serious about me or maybe I wasn't serious about those convictions. But he finally dumped me after a weekend we spent together when it became obvious that it wasn't going to happen. I'm glad it didn't, because, you know…fuck that dude. Or rather, don't.

Now that it looked like I might be catching real feelings for Scott, my flight reflex kicked in. Keeping him around could mean I might have to do some real relationship work. It was easier just to have a few dates and a bad ending, after which I'd create a mean *Sex and the City* bad-boyfriend name for the guy and go back to whining about being single.

But Scott was perfect that night. I wanted to hold his hand, but I didn't want to make the first move. Once Natalie Cole started to sing "Lollipops and Roses" with the orchestral strings and twirly lyrics lifting into the suddenly enchanted air, there were magnets in my fingertips, and a sweet warmth drew my hand into his, folded solidly on his side of the armrest, as if to claim it.

It was the most sensual thing I had ever experienced, and I very much wanted everyone around us to vaporize. I wanted the show to be over so we could go make out in the car. I could not wait to get back to the garage, to have him lean over to me, as I knew he would, firmly grasp the back of my coat, press me to the driver's side of my Scion, and...

"It was a bad kiss!" I said despairingly about fifteen minutes later, sinking into Stephanie and Lauren's couch. I'd jumped into my car and headed over to their house unannounced, in need of commiseration and maybe some sense slapped into me. They handed me a glass of wine and got ready to listen. I didn't get it. After so much heat, so much desire leading up to it, it all went...floopy. The kiss was too eager. Uncomfortably gummy.

"God is laughing at me." I groaned, then drank more wine because I was at a frustrating emotional loss and because wine is good. "I finally like a guy and he likes me and there's so much buildup and the kiss was bad."

"Maybe he's a bad kisser," Lauren said, "or maybe you overthought it and you need to shut up and get out of your head."

I was slightly defeated, but I didn't weasel out of the real first date-date the next night. I think my lips were trying to trip me up, but I refused to let them. Instead, I agreed to have an undeniably romantic dinner at an expensive vegetarian restaurant called Sublime. It was in Fort Lauderdale about forty-five minutes from my house, and I think it was my idea to meet him in the parking lot of the Whole Foods in Boca, closer to his place and sort of halfway between my place and the restaurant, as if that made it less of a hassle for him in case it went wrong. Scott was waiting with a dozen red roses and a container of organic lollipops, just like Natalie Cole had sung about, in the driver's seat of his red Bronco. And then we went to that very expensive vegetarian restaurant because I was mostly vegetarian, even though he was 100 percent carnivorous. He held my hand under the table, stroking my palm until I didn't mind letting the dessert melt.

After dinner he opened the passenger-side door of the Bronco for me, like a gentleman, and when he closed it, I remember counting the steps he was taking to the driver's side so he could get in and kiss me again. *It has to be better,* I chanted silently in my head. *It better be.*

Scott got in, leaned over, and the anticipation, the lingering, deliberate slowness with which his lips met mine, made me feel like I was dissolving into a puddle on the front seat of this Ford Bronco. *Oh my.* This was better than any kiss ever. It overshot its promise and soared straight into overachiever territory. It deserved a gold star. All the damn gold stars.

As I was reeling in the reality of this feeling that was dissolving my face, Scott touched my cheek, smiling softly, and said, all husky-like, "We have to go away somewhere really special the first time we make love."

It is hard to sound sincere and not super-corny when saying the words *make love,* but there in that car, as I floated in that puddle of desire and unexpected connection, it was perfect. Of course my ass was gonna have to ruin it.

"I should probably tell you," I said, pulling back ever so slightly, "that I am not intending to actually have sex until I am married, and we're probably not going to get married, so if that's a problem, you should know now."

This was part truth, part defense mechanism, and as much as I wanted to surrender completely to this kiss, I expected him to pause or say, *Deal-breaker! Let's get you back to your car...and whatever else you got going on without me.*

Dude didn't even flinch.

"That's okay," he said, leaning over to kiss me again.

Well, *that* was unexpected.

"Wait, did you hear me?" I said, and—*Oh my God, Leslie, shut up.* "I said I'm not going to be sleeping with you."

"I heard you," he said. And then he kept kissing me.

Well, then! Much later, after we were married and very much having sex, I asked him why that didn't scare him off.

"Because I knew I was going to marry you," Scott said. "And you were worth the wait."

I am sharing more than I'm sure Scott would want me to. But it's because I'm trying to do him justice, and it's important to consider that full-of-life man in his late thirties with the good kisses and the spicy words went on a year-long sex break influenced by a religion he did not follow because the woman he loved asked him to. That's it. Again, Scott might be embarrassed that I shared that. Forgive me, sweetheart. You can yell at me next time you see me.

5

You the Wife?

Listen, ma'am," says the very patient paramedic.

He's just materialized behind me in our dark driveway, where I am on the phone trying to explain to my mother that something very bad is happening to Scott. I don't know how long I've been out here or how long it took the ambulance to arrive. I can't even tell you how long the paramedics have been working on my husband, who, through the window, I can see lying face-up on the dining-room floor with determined, helpful men doing chest compressions on him. Down the hall, behind them, our baby, Brooks—who I am remembering has a social worker visit planned today, part of the process of our legally trying to adopt him—is hopefully still asleep. He loves firemen and has no idea that there are several in his house right now. That might disappoint him if he finds out, but I'm glad he's sleeping through it. I wish I were sleeping through it.

"Mommy, I have to go, the paramedic wants to talk to me," I say to my mother, trying to sound calm and convince her, helpless on the other end of the phone in Little Rock, that everything's all right. This looks bad but I want her to believe—*I* want to believe—that this is an emergency that's going to turn out okay. Denial is a hell of a drug.

And I can tell by the sweet paramedic's face that it's not okay. Nothing is. He takes a deep breath and starts a spiel I can tell he has given too many times.

"We have been working on your husband for a while, and there is no electrical activity in his heart, and we have to do his breathing for him. We're gonna do all we can do, but you should maybe start calling your family and your spiritual adviser."

"No electrical activity," I repeat, as if there weren't a lot of other important and terrible words and concepts in that sentence. He nods. He knows I don't know what to do, that my brain is protecting me by not immediately processing what he's telling me.

"Spiritual adviser," I say, and behind the sweet paramedic, my front door swings open and they're hurriedly carrying Scott on a stretcher to the ambulance. I can't see his face because it's covered in a mask, but there are reflections of red and blue lights streaking onto the brick pavers of the driveway. I want to throw up.

Because nobody brings up the damn spiritual adviser if there's any hope.

Nice Paramedic seems to know I'm not absorbing all of this, but he's got a job to do, so he also instructs me to call a friend to come and take me to the ER and to get someone to watch the baby.

"Do not drive," he says, and I think, *I must look a mess. I must be a mess.*

I call Lauren and ask her to come with me. I know I have to also get someone to stay with Brooks, who's still sleeping away, not knowing that the world is disintegrating. I've already called Lynne, in Annapolis, and I feel bad for waking her up because there's nothing she can do right now. All I'm doing is worrying her. I'm afraid we should all be very worried.

Lauren doesn't pick up the first time I call, or the second or the third. (Later I find out that she had been butt-dialed a bunch over the evening and early morning by her boss, so when the phone kept ringing at three a.m., she assumed that was what was happening again.) But I keep calling, because I have to go to the hospital. I am helpless to stop what's happening to the love of my life. I can't even will anyone to pick up the stupid phone. I want to run in and grab my baby and jump into the ambulance with my husband but I have to wait for other people, and that makes me angry. This thing—whatever it is—is happening without my permission, and I'm so powerless that I can't even drive myself to the hospital.

I dial Lauren again, and when I get nothing, I call her husband's cell. Jon groggily picks up after about three rings, and I must blurt out something panicky because he and Lauren show up on my doorstep soon after, around the same time as my neighbor Liz. Liz and I are supposed to be taking a walk in a few hours with Brooks in his little stroller, and I swear I don't remember calling her, but she says I did. (Apparently I told her that Scott was dead, and could she come watch Brooks? I have no memory of that conversation and assume this was part of my brain's evolutionary instinct to start winding me into a cocoon of bubble wrap so I could just get through the next few days without breaking.)

I pull on a dress and carefully open Brooks's bedroom

door. He's still asleep. By now it's like four in the morning and any parent in their right mind wants her toddler to stay that way, but I have this weird need to pick him up, to hold that little body next to mine and absorb the energy of the one person in this house who doesn't yet know his father is dying. So I breathe him in one last time and then bring him down the hall and shove him into Jon's arms. Brooks wakes up and starts wailing like I've broken some spell. I'm crushed—it's crushing me—but we gotta go.

My aunt Debbie, the reverend, calls as Lauren drives us to the hospital to find whatever we're going to find, and she prays over the phone. I try to find some magic words that will pray away what I know is happening. I believe in magic and in God and in miracles. *I want a miracle. Please give me a miracle.*

When we get out of the car, the hospital parking lot is quiet, dark, and empty. It's *too* quiet—I want EMTs to be frantically rushing around, calling all the doctors and nurses and yelling "Stat!" and demanding crucial labs or whatever. I want them to be loud and busy saving Scott's life. I want there to still be hope.

But there's no one out there except for one police officer, who seems...impatient? Annoyed? What the hell is he annoyed for? I'm the one whose husband is…I don't even want to think it. Thinking it makes it true.

"You the wife?" he says. I swear to God, this is how he greets me. Not *Hello, ma'am,* or *Are you here for Scott Zervitz?* Nope. He comes at me so abruptly, so gruff out of the box, that I involuntarily chuckle. Not that it's funny.

"Did he just say, 'Are you the wife?'" I whisper to Lauren. (Later, it will be explained to me that when a relatively young person dies at home unattended by law enforcement or medical professionals, there is an investigation. Jon and Liz, who stayed behind, will tell me that another cop, who was very nice, came to the house. He asked some questions, took a look at Scott's medication, apologized profusely for everybody's loss, and left, apparently satisfied that whatever happened was a cruel twist of health issues and unfortunate circumstances.)

I don't yet know about Good Cop at my house dealing with my friends like human beings, but I've watched enough crime shows to recognize Bad Cop. This man does not treat me like a victim, like someone who needs comfort. He treats me like I stole something.

And it feels like a betrayal.

Maybe I met this deputy on a bad day. Or maybe he's just an ass. I don't know. I don't care. But he knows he's probably talking to a widow, and he can't even feign politeness. Bad Cop jerks his uniformed shoulder dramatically past the sliding doors, where a scared-looking man—the desk clerk, maybe—is waiting for us. At least *he* looks sorry.

"Mrs. Zervitz?" he says. I nod, grateful that at least this guy's not visibly pissed at me for troubling him with my tragedy.

"Okay. Please have a seat in that room," he says, pointing to a closed door to his right. *Oh, shit.*

"That's not good," I mumble to Lauren. "That's the Bad News Room. They didn't say, *Let us take you to your husband* or *The doctors will be right out to tell you about his condition.* They want to tell me something. Something bad."

At first, the Bad News Room door won't open; it's locked, because there's a doctor inside charging his phone and maybe taking a nap. I'm glad someone's getting some downtime! After he scurries out, another doctor, good-looking in a forgettable-TV way, comes in, flanked by a few other people in scrubs and white coats. I think that maybe they're students and I wonder if I am part of a very special teaching moment.

"What happened?" the doctor asks me. He is very upset.

Aren't you supposed to be telling me that? "Why don't *you* tell *me* what happened?" I say. Bad Cop is in the room too, glaring at me and intently listening for my answer. What is it with this guy? Do I know him? Did I give his band a bad review?

The doctor pauses, then explains that Scott was not responsive when he was brought in and appears to have had a cardiac event. He had not been breathing on his own, and they could not revive him.

Shit.

"So he's gone, then," I say. There, I've said it. My voice sounds steadier than my chest feels.

He's gone. He's gone. Oh, no.

Some niceties are said; some papers are signed. Someone hands me a plastic Ziploc bag with Scott's watch, wedding band, and delightfully gaudy gold chain inside.

He needs his watch, I think.

No, he doesn't, my brain says. *It's okay, sweetheart. You'll catch up.*

Now that I know what's happened to Scott, it's time to tell everyone else. I cannot imagine feeling more devastated than this, and I love all the people I need to call too much to make them feel this too. But I have to, so I do, dreading not only saying the words but also what will happen right before, when someone I love hears that phone ring and checks the time, knowing that nothing good ever happens in the middle of the night.

Besides my loved ones whose lives I am destroying, I make two other important calls. The first is to our adoption social worker in Maryland, who doesn't answer because it's hideously early. So I leave her a voice mail: "Scott has died, so please call me back and tell me this doesn't hurt my chances of keeping my kid." (That must have been hard to hear. I'm really sorry about that.)

I also talk to a lady from the funeral home whom I instantly love, mostly because she's nice to me and refers to Scott as "your husband," not "the deceased." I do not have similar love for the person I talk to after I hang up, a young woman who comes into the Bad News Room on some clerical mission. More questions, more paperwork. Fine, hand it over. But then she does something not fine at all. She looks at me, then at Lauren, then at me, then back at Lauren, and says to her, "Mrs. Zervitz?"

Well, damn.

This young, nervous woman—who happens to be black and who really doesn't want to be in here, because who would?—makes a very human assumption: that the white woman is the widow of the dead white man, and the black woman is the friend. It is not crazy to assume this, because this is usually the case.

However, nothing about this situation is usual, and we

can't be going around assuming shit. All she had to do was say "Mrs. Zervitz?" and see who answered. A different newly minted widow would have smiled sadly and said, "No, dear, that's me." I am not that widow. "Over here," I say sharply. I can see I've made her uncomfortable, but it's not my job to make her feel better about the stupid shit she just did. I see her eyes get wide, like a rabbit who's not only about to be eaten by a wolf but first has to wait for the wolf to list the many, many ways in which she's trifling.

"Are you *kidding* me? Even now, in this moment, I can't get someone to recognize my marriage. Great. Just lovely."

She shrinks back like she's about to cry, and I glance over at Lauren. Lauren is my ride-or-die, my personal chauffeur through hell; she watches me lay into this poor young woman, and she lets me do it. Not for nothing, but ten years ago, Lauren, who hadn't even been to a funeral when I met her, held my hand as my little crazy cat Cusack was put to sleep. She knows not only about this very present pain but about the stories she's heard about people assuming me and Scott weren't together, like when I asked a waiter to put us on the same check but he looked at Scott's white relatives across the table and told me he'd already separated the check "by family." Ow.

Lauren routinely puts herself between me and pain, and

here she is again, not trying to stop me as I let go on this poor, wrong young woman in this Bad News Room in this terrible hospital who is getting a bit of anger I'd bottled up and reserved from all the assholes who were ever mean to me and Scott. That's not fair. Right now, I don't care. I can't bring my baby back, but yelling at this poor girl is something I can do. I'm sorry, lady, if you're reading this. Do better, though.

"Is that all?" I ask, though it's not really a question; we are done. Clerk Girl hands over the form and skedaddles. Smart Clerk Girl. "Was I wrong?" I ask Lauren. She shakes her head—either she agrees with me or she doesn't want to get yelled at too. Smart Lauren.

The door opens again, and it's a nice nurse, one of the guys who was here with the doctor who told me Scott was dead. He tells me that he recognizes me from the newspaper and that, by the way, he likes my column. He is one of the first people in this awful place who has treated me like a human, and I'd like to hug him. Nice Nurse asks if I'd like to see Scott. Of course I would, because he's my love and I know I'll regret it if I say no. Lauren is suddenly next to me in the hallway.

"You don't have to come," I say, remembering that she's not as funeral-proficient as I am, but she hushes me.

"See," I say as we go to the room where my husband's body is, "you thought that coming with me to see the cat put to sleep was the worst thing I'd ever ask you to do."

"Absolutely. I'm never answering your calls again," she says, and I laugh, and then she does too. As fucked up as this all is, it's at least a little funny.

The door to the room where Scott is stands open and I don't want to do this. "I don't want to do this," I whisper to Lauren, or maybe Scott, or maybe God. But we all know I have to. I edge inside gingerly, hoping this was all a mistake. But it's not. There's my boy, eyes mostly closed, lying on a hospital bed, still wearing one of his sleep Ravens jerseys. It has been slit open so the EMTs could get to his chest.

"At least it wasn't one of your good jerseys, huh?" I say. His Maryland sports-jersey collection ranks somewhere in importance to him just below Brooks, me, and crab cakes.

He does not answer, and his inability to do so whips me around the temple.

Oh, Scott.

I feel a tug of despair, but it passes. Scott is not in this body, but he's in the room, maybe hovering around the air ducts, looking on in dismay at what's happened to his jersey.

"Hey, baby," I whisper, standing next to the gurney and

leaning down to kiss him on his forehead. He does not move when I kiss him, and I remember he won't, obviously, and I choke down the wail clawing up my throat because this is my last moment ever to talk to him like this. If Scott is in the rafters, I'm not fucking this up.

"We're gonna be okay, Scotty," I say, squeezing his shoulder. He does not move. "I promise. I'm gonna take care of Brooks, and we're gonna finish the adoption, and he's going to be ours, for real, okay? And we'll be okay, and we're gonna be happy, and it's gonna be okay. I promise. I love you. I'm so sorry. We're gonna be okay."

I don't really know how long we're in there. I wonder if it's long enough, because there is no do-over. I'm scared that I might be doing this wrong. *All of this is wrong.* But as I touch his bald head one last time, something solidifies in me instead of breaking. I am not okay. But I'm okay enough to do the next things I have to do. All of them will be awful.

We walk out of the room where the love of my life is lying dead and—stop, stop, it's too awful, stop.

6

Grief Cake

About ten hours before Scott died, he gave me some sake he'd bought at the gas station, because we were classy that way. Brooks was adorably drooling on his friends or toddling into furniture or whatever almost-two-year-olds do at day care, which we liked to call Baby School. (He was acing it.) Scott had been free that day—he had left his old tech sales job a couple of months earlier and was starting a new one in less than a week, so he'd been doing all those errands you frantically do during the last few days of vacation that you won't be able to do when you're back at work.

He'd spent the day at a flea market about an hour south

of us to buy clip-on sunglasses for his hard-to-fit prescription specs and peruse hard-to-find Baltimore sports memorabilia. His memorabilia addiction was a thing with us. Normally I was sort of a penny-pinching bitch about it because we had bills and a baby. Nobody needs tacky shit like the highlight of that particular day's haul: the most wretched tie-dyed Ravens shirt ever silk-screened in the bowels of hell's gift shop.

He also bought an Orioles polo shirt, which is still hanging in my closet because I can't bear to get rid of it, and some baseball cards for Brooks. To make up for the fact that he'd just spent too much money, he got me the autograph of the guy who worked in the sports memorabilia shop—he had, randomly, played a bit part in *The Last of the Mohicans*—and the aforementioned gas-station sake.

That was our pattern. When Scott thought I was going to be mad at him for spending more than a hundred bucks on some sports-related impulse buy, he always threw in something for me or the baby so I wouldn't be *as* mad. Of course, that gift added to the tally of money he'd spent that day, but it was usually something personal and sweet enough to slightly diminish my anger.

Slightly.

Happily, the sake worked like a cheap, boozy charm. It

was the gift equivalent of buying a magnet for your mom in the airport ten minutes before you board, but his thoughtfulness, and the delightful tackiness of it, took the edge off my anger. Yes, I'm a sucker. Also, he was so happy about this new job and this new chapter that I toned the penny-pinching down several notches and just accepted all the joy to come.

Sigh.

The very next day, when too many people are standing around somberly in my living room, I find the sake in the refrigerator, just where Scott left it. Drinking it seems like the right thing to do. And being sort of buzzed seems like a nice thing to be at this moment. So now I'm in the middle of my living room, barefoot and slugging sake out of the bottle. I'm sure it's a mess. Don't care. My sister, Lynne, sees me.

"Leslie!" she barks. "Stop that!"

Lynne, who loves my husband something fierce, is in her own state of shock, her own mourning haze, but at the moment, her unofficial role is She Who Holds It Together. The job requirements include making sure that I don't make a spectacle of myself or tarnish the family name. Normally, that might be important to me, but right now I don't much give a shit.

"My husband bought me this sake," I say, aware that I sound unhinged. "It's the last thing he ever bought me, and I. Am. Going. To. Drink. It."

Lynne's eyes—Scott always referred to them as Disney princess–like—widen in shock. I feel awful, as no one ever wants to hurt Princess Jasmine's feelings, and I also know that I have spent my life caring about how my feelings affected other people. But right now, I only have to care about what I want.

And what I want to do is drink this damn sake.

We are entering an awful, awful period. The Grief Cake period, so named for all of the cake and booze and carbs and *anything not nailed down* that I will consume. During the next two months, I will gain ten pounds, stop sleeping, and become way too familiar with the staff at the dive bar across the street, right next to the pie shop. As well as with the staff at the pie shop.

Everyone is going to notice, everyone is going to worry, but most are going to let it go because the shittiest thing in the world has happened to me. No one knows how to make it right, and they can't crawl into my grief with me because they can't and because nobody would want to because it smells like booze and feet and old cake in here.

And during this blessed, messy Grief Cake period, I'm

not all that picky about the source of the indulgence. My friend Melanie, who materializes in Florida the night Scott dies, keeps showing up with presents throughout that awful week, like a gift-bearing sprite. At one point, she's next to me with a bottle of Fireball whiskey, the little devil on the label peeking out of the brown paper bag she's holding. Fireball, to me, tastes like Red Hots and vengeance, so I'm skeptical it will help.

"You look like a wino," I say as she opens the creaky screenless screen door to our backyard and beckons me to follow her. "We really gonna be out here slugging Fireball out of a paper bag with all these people in the house?"

Mel smiles, chugs a chug, and hands it to me. "Yes, we are. And who the hell would blame you right now? You can do whatever the hell you want."

The lady has a point. "Isn't Fireball a thing for drunk twenty-one-year-olds?"

"I'm sure it is," she says. "And when you drink it, it'll be a thing for sad forty-four-year-olds."

I look inside at all the people milling around, trying to be useful and take away at least a little of this mountain of hurt. And then I look back at my friend trying to do the same thing with this ridiculous bottle. I'm tired of thinking, of being sad.

I take a slug.

"Oww!" I wipe my mouth like I've been bitten. "That's awful."

"Well, in my defense, *I* like it," Melanie says, taking her bottle back. "And now you feel something, don't you?"

Yes. I feel like someone just blasted liquefied cinnamon into my lungs with a blowtorch. But it beats abject misery.

I am officially the Crazy Widow Zervitz, so how can I be expected to act normal? Normal is toast. I'm in new, unstable territory, eating and drinking and sobbing my way through whatever the hell is happening to me. I'll be greeting guests and thanking them for coming over like I'm hosting brunch, then I'll abruptly end conversations with "I'm sorry, I have to go now," so I can run up the hall to lie down in the dark, because if I don't escape I'm going to disintegrate or slap folks.

I'm becoming way too comfortable with feeling out of control. I know that I should be more polite, less buzzed, more present. But I can't do it. And I'm sort of sorry about it, but...really, I'm not that sorry.

When Brooks is not in Baby School, he's either gleefully being spoiled by all these surprise visitors or sleeping soundly in his crib in the next room, still with no clue what's happening. I'm jealous. I, too, would love to be a clueless sleeping baby. I know that some of the worried people watching over me are also watching him. This is not a good look. Can't take care of myself. Can't take care of my own kid. Can't even sleep or give my brain permission to just shut up. I'm kinda useless.

I am so thankful for Baby School, where Brooks has a lot of friends and is beloved and popular. He's not quite two, and he's been raised by Mr. Life of the Party, and that charm has rubbed off. They don't look a thing alike, but when you see Scott and Brooks together—and they're always together, with Mommy walking behind with the baby bag like the nanny—you know they're father and son. Soul mates. The last time Brooks saw Daddy, he was carrying him to bed after dinner and telling him about the history of wrestling. I believe he'd gotten up to Dusty Rhodes.

Now they'll never get to finish that lesson, and everything's up to me, including the WWF/WWE transition and, more important, explaining what the hell is going on now. I know Brooks knows that something's weird because all of these people are in his house and Scott isn't.

"How do I tell him this?" I ask Melanie, a veteran mother and educator.

"Hell if I know," she says. I'm so glad she's here!

I really don't know what I'm going to tell the baby. I

never imagined being a widow before the age of, like, sixty-five—until my daddy died, I never really thought about widowhood at all. But my mom joined the club at sixty-four, way before she was supposed to, so every once in a while, I'd look at Scott chewing on a rib or taking all of his meds at once because he'd skipped them for a week and thought to say, "Please take care of yourself. Please don't leave me."

And he'd smile his crooked smile and say, "Where am I gonna go?"

I have never wanted to yell *I told you so* at a dead person before. There's a first for everything, I guess.

I don't remember everything that happens in the first week or so after Scott died. Grief doesn't break just your heart—it breaks your brain. It dents your body, hobbles your ability to take full breaths. I ask my sister to make sure I don't lose it on anyone but remind her that as the Widow Zervitz, I am allowed to talk shit about those people when they're not there. Grief. My brain, you know.

I feel bad for my family and friends and even all the people across the country who leave stunned, lovely tributes to Scott on various Facebook pages because no one knows what to say. Nothing is really going to be comforting other than *The hospital made a huge mistake and we're driving Scott*

77

back to your house, but everyone is trying. For the next few days I will note what makes me sort of smile and what makes me stabby. I mostly like when people post *Oh, no!* or *Leslie, I loved Scott and am so sorry for your loss.* What *isn't* helpful is any suggestion, especially in the first day or so, that Scott is now an angel or that he is in a better place or that, as one person writes, *Scott has completed his cycle on Earth.* Gross.

Look, I know that these people are trying to make sense of a senseless thing, offering a nice blanket statement of comfort to cover me. But I can still smell Scott's aftershave on my blanket. The place he was in just hours ago, where he's supposed to be now, is this old recliner, not Heaven. Heaven is probably better, décor-wise. But he's supposed to be here with me. Not anywhere else. It's not fair, but I suspect that when people say, "Well, he's happy in eternity," it's about making themselves feel better. I hope it works for them, because it's not working for me.

For most of my life, I have been the comforter, the friend that people come to for some sort of wisdom, even if my own choices were sometimes suspect or even stupid. But now, in this Grief Cake period, the roles have switched. I am the one needing comfort; I am Comfort Ground Zero.

When my daddy died, I couldn't stop looking over at my mom, the person least removed from that pain. She couldn't run, couldn't hide. And I thought, *I never want to be that person. I need someone else's grief to hide behind.* Three years later, *I* am the widow. Didn't see that coming! I am now the pitied, the one everyone's watching, the way they do on *Law & Order,* to make sure she's grieving properly. I have to hold the hands of people who don't know what to say, who want to hug me while my body's physically recoiling from over-hugging, when I need to run.

Why do I feel guilty? This thing just happened—happened *to me*—but already I'm fearing that moment where everyone is sick of me, when I'll have spent my pity allowance. You know, like when you were younger, and your friends had bad breakups, and everyone was really patient and easy on them for a few days, maybe even a week or two if the ex was being particularly ass-y? For a little while, you expected them to be weepy, to start every conversation with "I can't believe Ryan broke up with me!" or try to sneak his name into every conversation, like "So when we get ice cream, can we not drive by that 7-Eleven where Ryan bought me that ginger ale on my birthday?" Girl. You dated that guy for like three weeks and we're still talking about him?

It's not *The Notebook.*

I was with Scott for a lot longer than three weeks, and I don't think I'm being unreasonably dramatic here, but I'm still afraid of being too much, of doing too much, of bumming everyone out with my inconvenient sadness. I don't want to be the widow who's a burden. I don't want to be the widow at all. But I am never *not* going to be a widow.

Over the next several days, I will occasionally be so overwhelmed with grief and my wine buzz that I'm slapped unconscious and just fall asleep. I usually have no idea what time it is—there's no clock in my room, and someone has taken my phone away from me so I can rest. But that just means I'm really alone, not just physically but really, really cosmically alone.

The morning after Scott dies, when I can't lie still anymore or stand to be alone for one more second, I wander, zombie-like, down the hallway while I'm supposed to be resting. *Resting,* in this instance, really means just staring wide-eyed at the empty side of the bed in the horrible quiet. I float down to the living room to see who's down there, because my house has become a morbid Christmas special—you never know who the next guest star is gonna be!

"Go lie down!" somebody says, sternly but with love. I've been avoiding mirrors, big-time, so I have no idea what I look like, but I assume it's not good, like Macy Gray as the Bride of Frankenstein. But I defiantly plop down—I think on the floor—and explain that I wasn't sleeping anyway, and I want to be around people, at least until my body tells me to jump up like I've been Tased and flee back down the hall.

Rinse, cry, repeat.

I'm still counting the time Scott's been gone in hours, not days. I don't want to make anyone feel bad. These are all normal, nice people, many of whom bought plane tickets and took time off work to come down here so they'll be here to catch me if I happen to fall apart. I'm especially impressed with my fellow newsroom folks, who start streaming through my living room at a steady clip not long after we get back from the ER. I still don't know where my phone is, which is unusual for me. Maybe whoever took it from me put it back in my purse? Somewhere in that same purse is Scott's watch, in that sad plastic bag given to me by one of the nurses, along with his wedding band.

Where is it? I need to go dump my whole purse out till I find the phone so I can punch around and find the video of Brooks surfing on Scott's knee as they watch the opening credits of *Hawaii Five-O*, Brooks's smushy toddler face so focused, Scott trying his best not to crack up. His boy is serious and he's not going to disrespect him. I want to listen to whatever mundane message Scott last left me, because I desperately need to hear his voice. But starting a grand search around my house with all these people here is just going to make me look more pathetic, more worrisome, and they are going to tell me to rest. And I. Can't. Stand. It.

The mourners keep coming, drawn by some Grief Bat Signal (or maybe Facebook). For a person once described by a former boss as "very good at being the center of attention," I don't love being fussed over right now. I do like the pity nachos, though. But when everyone rushes to your side after your husband dies, you can't just pretend it's not a big deal. It is the *biggest* of deals. It's like a bad breakup, but one where God does the breaking up for you.

I'm not sure what to expect of this week, other than that it's going to be awful. I know this might be hard to follow, but timelines keep slipping—I don't always know what day it is or who's gotten to Florida yet or what anyone is supposed to be doing. All I know is that I can't get back to the timeline I'd prefer, the one where Scott's still alive and all these people can go the hell home.

What I do know is that I will feel loved and supported and then everyone will go home and Scott will still be dead. Lynne tells me later that during the first couple of days, I thank people a lot—maybe too much. I don't quite remember, just like I don't remember how I told people that Scott was dead. We were supposed to go visit our friend Abbey in Key West for Scott's forty-fifth birthday, and when I call her either the day he died or the day after to tell her the news, she thinks I'm calling to confirm our visit. Later, Abbey tells me that I said, "So, the thing is, Scott died." Just like that.

I am supposed to be focusing on me and Brooks right now—I really need to talk to that social worker—so there will be time to worry about other stuff. These people around us have willingly and selflessly jumped into the messiness with me. But I am vaguely aware that I'm hurting people, like Abbey, just by being the one who says the words "Scott is dead." I hope they forgive me.

Scott died on a Wednesday morning, and if I were a good Jewish wife, or even the good wife of a Jew, he'd have been buried within twenty-four hours, forty-eight max. But I'm a Baptist, and many of my deceased loved ones have been left peacefully sitting on ice for more than a week while Aunt What's-Her-Name and Uncle Whosit get their money together and get time off work. Scott always thought that was weird.

"What, are you keeping them in the freezer until it fits into your schedule?" he'd say.

"Uh, yeah," I'd say. "It's okay. He'd want Cousin What's-His-Face to be there!"

By the time we rally the troops—so many more troops than I'd imagined—it's too close to Friday night, and the Jewish funeral home won't bury him until Sunday morning at the earliest. So that's what we'll do. By that time, I've heard that there are a bunch of people coming down later, after the funeral. I'm going to need people to be here after the crowds all leave and the only ones left are the die-hards, like the fans who hang out after the encore hoping the band comes back for one more song. Except the band is just one sad bleary chick with an open bottle of cheap-ass sake and nothing but time. You couldn't pay anyone to see that show. Yet here they are. So here is your show.

I can't vouch for the after-party.

7

Try Not to Ruin Your Romantic Weekend by Throwing Up Too Much

About two years after Scott dies, I attend the Tampa edition of an annual international conference called Camp Widow. It's very much about widows but not at all about camping, because I don't ever camp, and as much as I want to heal, I never want to heal *that* bad.

Camp Widow is where widowed people of every gender, race, age, and geographic location come to just be, to fall apart or share or help each other or laugh about dark widow shit that nobody else gets. I meet a very wise woman named Tanya whose firefighter fiancé, Sergio, died on 9/11, and she tells me the most hopeful thing: At first, it destroyed her to think that her fiancé would never make new memories. But as she began to tell their story to those who didn't know him, to talk about things they did and who he was, she realized that a whole new group of people had now been introduced to him, that they now had new memories of Sergio. He'll live on in those stories with these new people.

Isn't that gorgeous? So in that spirit, here's the story of the first time I told Scott I loved him. It would have eventually happened anyway but happened to happen in an expensive room at the Mandarin Oriental in Miami, so it's extra-cinematic. Scott won two nights in the hotel and a spa package in a silent auction at a celebrity dance competition, where I came in third. I was wearing a neon-green spandex situation, along with a pair of Spanx that not only didn't suck anything in but pushed my fat up into an extra shiny shelf of even more fat. Sequined neon fat.

"Dancing with the Spanx" would prove to be significant for a few reasons. It was the first time Scott met my mom, who hadn't quite realized how serious we were. I'd been playing my feelings so close to the vest that they were practically embroidered onto the vest. It was also the day that Scott made it clear just how permanent his feelings for me were, announcing that he'd spent the afternoon looking for an apartment near me. So, it was getting *real*. Perhaps too real.

At the time, Scott was still bunking with his cousins in Boca Raton, about half an hour away from me. I wasn't really interested in long-term dating someone who didn't have his own place—he was at my condo a lot, mostly chastely, because I was sticking to my celibacy guns. But I didn't want him living with me officially until we were married. That was partially due to my own convictions, but also because I didn't want to disappoint my family. They were several states away, so I could have just lied to them, but that would have created one of those sitcom situations where you forget whom you lied to when, and then your grandma's coming over while you're hiding a man in the shower. I didn't have time to floss; I certainly didn't have time to keep track of all that.

I now somewhat regret that as much time as Scott spent at my place, I didn't let him and all of his jerseys officially move in early because I was a grown woman who didn't like admitting that she was still making major life choices based on other people's approval.

Because I was previously bad at relationships, I was hesitant to accept that his residential plans had anything to do with me, so I was sort of a punk about it—"Are you moving up closer to me because of me or because that's where you want to live just because you like it?" I asked.

"Because of you," Scott said matter-of-factly, then went back to whatever it was he was doing.

"What if we don't work out?"

I could have blown this. Fortunately, Scott was not to be swayed by my rookie skittishness.

"We'll work out," he said, because he was such a confident guy, such a go-down-with-his-ship sort, at least when it came to us. Sometimes it seemed foolhardy. But we all gotta go down sometime, so it might as well be together.

(While we're on the subject, it's a good time to remind you that since we all do go down sometime, as in get sick and die, you should always listen to your doctors and take your prescribed medications.)

Right before the dance competition, Scott told me and my mom about an apartment he'd seen that afternoon near the Port of Palm Beach, maybe fifteen minutes from my condo. It had seemed like a nice older home and a possibility until the woman showing it to him pointed to a painting on the wall. In my imagination it was one of those haunted-house portraits with the eyes that follow you like on *Scooby-Doo*. The woman in the painting was the home's former owner, who, the friend showing the house said, was right this minute haunting and watching over the place to make sure it was being rented to the right person. Also, the eventual tenant was going to have to take care of the deceased's cat, Mr. Christmas. Enjoy your haunted house and cat!

"Are you gonna go visit Scott if he takes that apartment?" my mom whispered.

"Oh, hell no," I said, planning to talk him out of it. I did love him, however, so I'm sure if he'd taken it I'd have been over there with Mr. Christmas and the haunted painting soon enough. Love makes you do dumb shit.

I look at photos of me at the dance competition now, with my disco-ball trophy that was literally a disco ball Super-Glued into a trophy cup and my lime-green double fat, and it makes me laugh. My real prize was this man. I had yet to cop to that last part, but it was coming. Soon.

Getting to stay at the Mandarin felt special because I had been there for press junkets to interview famous movie people. I once sat across from the Rock on a balcony as his publicist tried to cut my interview short so some TV people had more time. (To his credit, he wouldn't let her.) And there was that time Daniel Craig, arm in a sling, opened one of those tiny hospitality Diet Cokes with his good hand and I can't remember most of the interview because I think

I might have passed out with my eyes open. My knees were actually sweating under my tall leather pirate boots. Daniel Craig makes your knees sweat. It's science!

As often as I'd worked there, I had never gotten to stay overnight in my own room like a normal rich person, because I am not a rich person, normal or otherwise. So when Scott showed me the gift certificate, my brain went fuzzy and I was so excited that I found a special place on my foyer table to put it so I wouldn't forget it. And then, of course, we drove two hours to the hotel and forgot it. The fancy front-desk clerk at the Mandarin politely explained that she would need to see the actual piece of paper and we were gonna have to either produce it or Groupon it back two hours up the highway in a rainstorm. Fortunately, our neighbors, who were feeding my cat that weekend, had a fax machine and sent it to the hotel. The day, and our free weekend, was saved!

The fancy room itself wasn't much bigger than a normal one, but it seemed special somehow. There were some tasteful gold accents, and shiny wood, and some sort of perfectly subtle elegant smell that you'd have to qualify for financially to buy. I immediately sank into the bed and kicked my shoes off, because shoes are oppressive and a tool of the Man.

Maybe it was the power of the free fancy room, but I could feel distinct words forming on my tongue. I'd been denying them for a while, denying even thinking them, although I did mention them in passing to Lynne, but we're twins so she probably figured it out anyway. I didn't intend to be the first one to say what I now *needed* to say—I had promised myself that I was not going to be. It's a vulnerable thing to expose your tender heart to the elements or to the one who could reject you. And since Scott had assumed the role of the sure one, the pursuer, I wanted to sit back in that tower that his assurances had built for me. If he said it first, I'd know it meant that he was more sure than I was and would therefore never leave me.

But we were sitting on that perfect hotel bed, and Scott was smiling like a goofball, and the light was hitting that precious bald head just right. The words were fighting each other to be the first to break free of my mouth. I wasn't sure they were going to be in the right order even if I could stop them. I was shocked at how much I didn't want to.

"I love you," I said, and the smile threatened to run off his face clear to his ears.

"I love you too."

"Damn," I said. "I wanted you to say it first."

"Yeah, I know," Scott said. "I decided I was going to wait until you did it."

Sometimes when you love someone and he says something infuriating, it's cute.

We made out till dinner, then floated down to the super-nice and pricey hotel sushi restaurant, watching boats bobbing by on the dark, glassy Biscayne Bay, and I wanted to shout at them, *Hey, rich sailing people! I love this man and he loves me!*

Because sushi is not as filling as, like, a big-ass waffle, I was still hungry when we love-floated back upstairs. I woke up even hungrier but didn't eat because we had our couples massage scheduled for that morning, and I didn't want a big breakfast that would sit in my stomach like an eggy brick. I was also admittedly self-conscious about not being a wafer-thin rich white girl in this hotel that seemed to be manufacturing them in the spa's basement.

So, yeah...I didn't eat before our five-hour spa day and didn't drink enough water either. I appreciate now that this was a rookie mistake but back then, I just figured I was preventing unattractive belly bloat.

This would prove to be super-dumb.

By the time the friendly masseuses got us into the fluffy robes in the tasteful dimly lit massage room, the *Sounds of*

Vaguely Ethnic Stillness playing tastefully in the background, all I could feel was fluff and love. At some point, someone asked if we wanted to add some more time onto our massage, and we were like, "Sure!" because we hadn't paid for the base massage and how much more could it be? Also, we were in love! Love is love! Love is more important than money! Who needs money?

We would, apparently. Love, it seems, renders one unable to do math.

This complete disregard for frivolities like prices continued for the rest of the day, starting with that couples massage, where we were so into each other, beaming across the room from our separate tables, that we didn't mind being naked and flabby with strangers' hands on us. The gift certificate was on the books and we were in love; what could go wrong? I had a mani-pedi scheduled, and someone asked if we wanted an upgrade, and we were like, "Sure!" I was so melty that I would have agreed to anything just to keep all the melting going. That's how they get you. I am, again, from hood-adjacent Baltimore and pride myself on not being gettable.

Fool!

The mani-pedi was the beginning.

We basically went through the day just nodding to

stuff. I don't think there were dollar signs written on the brochures for the things that we were agreeing to with those happy sheep nods. But I was not remembering the most important lesson of Sheila E.'s "The Glamorous Life," which is "If you have to ask, you can't afford the lingerie."

We did not ask. We could not afford the lingerie. Or the extra eleventy-three hours of spa treatments. We did not realize that until we floated on that spa love cloud from the nail salon into the checkout area, where they handed us the bill in a tasteful black leather book. We figured it would be a couple hundred more on top of what we got with the gift certificate.

We were wrong. So wrong.

"Umm, did they actually apply the gift certificate?" I whispered, because there were too many commas and zeros on that bill. "They know we have a gift certificate, right?"

Some people would have just handed over their credit cards and shuffled out into the light to find a dollar menu because the fancy-food budget was blown. Those people are not from Baltimore.

Instead, Scott calmly explained that it hadn't been made explicitly clear to us how much all this adding and extending and nodding would cost, and if there was any way that we could have some of those extra numbers taken off, because those offers came when we were already naked and spilled out on the table like blissful sea slugs, that would be great. Not all of them; just a reasonable amount. And it worked! We thanked them and left before whoever approved that changed their mind. Thanks, whoever!

I got a good man, I thought as we sat down, woozy and subdued from our victory and all that spa work, to eat some lunch. Remember when I said that I was dehydrated and hungry before we even got to the massage? Fun fact: Massages dehydrate you. More. And doing all that on an empty stomach and then introducing french fries, sushi, and red wine all at once into that stomach is not a good idea.

After lunch, we took a nap. Actually, *nap* is too gentle a word for what my body did—the sensation was more like being stomped on by an elephant with velvet feet. When I woke up, I was somehow hungry again, so we decided to go try an Italian restaurant within walking distance of the hotel. I still felt sort of weird, but I figured there was nothing fancy pasta wouldn't fix.

You know that moment when it's definitely, unavoidably clear that you are going to be sick? When you feel that tiny wormy sensation at the pit of your gut snaking its way up faster than you can quell it, and the only question is whether you have time to get to the bathroom? That moment came at that romantic Italian restaurant as I was sitting across from my beloved. I was about four bites into my pasta, which of course tasted like what harp-playing angels sound like. I mumbled that I'd be right back and scampered as sweetly as I could to the ladies' room. It's hard to be elegant when you're about to hurl. But I tried.

I managed to make it to the bathroom in time, but its level of fanciness made me feel even worse, because I was super-self-conscious about throwing up there and tried to at least do it neatly. I was thinking about poor Scott out there in the middle of the dining room and wondering if people were looking at the empty chair across from him, assuming he got ditched. I imagined there were, at that moment, nice Jewish ladies discreetly slipping him their single granddaughters' numbers and murmuring, "I don't see a ring yet. It's not too late."

As I sat there, trapped in that upscale bathroom, I thought about how I wanted Scott to love me enough that instead of grossing him out, this episode would be the funny story we told at our wedding reception and at our twenty-fifth-anniversary party. I was living in a *Sex and the City* episode. Like, I couldn't help but wonder: *Is he ever going to stop looking at me and thinking about puke?*

When I finally made my shaky way back to the table, I started apologizing for ruining this perfect moment, but Scott wouldn't hear it. "It's not your fault you got sick," he said. Well, it kinda was, with the lack of hydration and the sushi and all, but this lovely man was letting me off the hook, so it was my job to just shut up, be gracious, and try not to throw up on anything else. We went back to the fancy hotel room, but instead of making out with Scott for hours as planned, I spent the night curled up in a ball, Scott giving me sips of water and rubbing my back.

By the next morning, I was feeling not only better but also very hungry. My stomach hadn't learned a thing. My full container of pasta was just sitting there on the dresser, but the fancy restaurant had failed to throw in any plastic silverware. That's a mistake that the black ladies who serve the fish dinners down at the AME church never make.

I figured I could sneak out, go downstairs to the lobby, and try to beg a fork off somebody, or I could just be the resourceful, strong woman Scott had fallen in love with.

About ten minutes later, he woke up and found his re-sourceful, strong beloved perched on the edge of the bed with her fancy hands shoveling penne into her mouth, and he didn't flinch. He just grabbed his phone and called his cousin Kenny.

"Kenny," he said. "Your future cousin is a foul beast."

He wasn't wrong about the foul part. But he'd also said "future cousin." So, foul or not, I was in.

8

Bashert

When we became parents, Scott and I got all sorts of advice, most of it well meaning, some of it judge-y, some of it completely damn useless. I'd heard one of the most useful bits more than twenty years before Brooks was born, when I was still single. From Tom Cruise.

Okay, so he didn't personally advise me, but Mr. Mission Impossible did say something decades ago in an interview that's now my template for parenting a child who had a life, however brief, before he came to be my son. When Tom and his then-wife, Nicole Kidman, adopted their son, Connor, reporters and other nosy folks were interested in his background not only because he was now the son of megastars but also because he was biracial. Tom's answer was that Connor's story was Connor's to tell when—or if—he decided to do so. The kid had his own history that predated his life as Connor Cruise, and it wasn't the right of his parents or anyone else to share that with *Entertainment Tonight*.

So I have decided to follow Tom Cruise's lead—a sentence I have never typed before—in that I don't talk much about Brooks's life before he came to be Brooks. That's his business. I believe that Scott and I were meant to be his parents, and he's an incredibly handsome baby, but he's not a plot device in my heartbreaking but eventually uplifting story. Brooks is a human being who is one day going to Google himself—or using whatever we'll be using to look up random information in the future—and I don't want him knocking on my door in the middle of the night yelling, *You wrote* what *about me?*

I also want to add that when I say that Brooks was meant to be with me, it's not because I'm one of those narcissistic adoptive parents who tell their kids they were carried in the wrong bellies or some gross shit like that. Birth parents aren't a footnote. They aren't the cabbage patch or anonymous storks. Optimally, kids should be raised by the people who conceived them, but sometimes that isn't possible. So those kids deserve to be raised by people who can take good care of them. That's what Scott and I, two almost-middle-aged people who wanted a kid, tried to do.

By the time we were a couple, I was at the age when a pregnancy would be labeled "geriatric." That's harsh, but science does not care about your old-ass feelings. We'd been discussing parenthood since we started dating, and we were old as hell even then. By the time we got married, a year later, I was three months from my thirty-ninth birthday, and Scott was seven months from his fortieth.

Even so, we decided we weren't going to try for a few months, wanting to luxuriate in marital bliss and whatnot and also enjoy having sex, which turned out to be worth the wait. Looking back, I wonder if I'd have waited if I'd known we would only have five years to be married and together in that way. You can only make decisions based on the information you have at the moment, and it doesn't help anyone to beat yourself up over it. I just wish we'd had more time.

We started trying for a baby in earnest not long after Scott's mother, Sharon, died, six months after we got married. It seemed slightly desperate, like a reaction to our mortality. Maybe it was. But given subsequent events, we weren't wrong, were we? Even as we tried to have a baby the old-fashioned way, we also considered adopting, whether or not we had a child biologically. We both had adopted children in our families, and that just seemed like a thing that you did.

Sharon, who had two lovely granddaughters and wanted to be a grandmother again as soon as Scott stepped on the glass at our wedding, actually tried to find us a baby—a family friend was pregnant and was considering adoption. She wound up keeping her child, and Sharon said, "We'll find you another one," like it was so easy. And, girl, you know it's not.

Sometimes fate makes the decision for you. Fate and being geriatric, I suppose, because I was *not* getting pregnant. For an upbeat person, Scott could sometimes be pessimistic when it came to things he wanted; he talked about literal generational curses he believed had been visited upon his family "back in the old country." He wasn't sure which old country, but it was "either Russia or Poland." He was sure of that.

Whatever the genesis of the supposed curse, Scott assumed that my not getting pregnant was all his fault and he added *Cannot get wife pregnant* to his list of supposed failures. I suggested we go get tested before we just gave up and blamed it on a curse. We started with blood tests. But the first one was inconclusive, and time got away from us, and we never did go back to find out just what the problem was.

Because that's when people started dying.

I'm not exaggerating. We had a whole season of death— several seasons, really—and now the cast of *Rent* is here to sing a peppy, meaningful song about them. Scott's mom died in 2010, on Labor Day, and then Scott's *bubbe* got very ill, and she died too. And my dad's cancer, which he'd been fighting since 2008, was back and vengeful.

Every time we thought we finally had time to regroup and put our minds back on the baby game, new shit happened. The business Scott worked for was failing. The cat was sick. Money was tight. Daddy was still not good and it was heartbreakingly clear that he was not going to get better. The air-conditioning in our condo went out, and we had the most ridiculous series of fights. I wish we'd spent that time working out a savings plan or volunteering at a soup kitchen or at least having more sex. Hindsight and all.

I asked the doctors when it would be a good time to try again, but they were basically like, *Um, shit seems to be raining down on you like retribution from on high, so you might first want to apologize for whatever you did to God and fix that, because it appears you're screwed.*

Actually, they simply advised us to wait until things calmed down. Ha-ha. We still thought maybe we might just get pregnant, but sickness and brokenness are not sexy, and it was too damned hot for cuddling that summer, what with our broken AC. And people kept dying: The Reverend Lester, my granddaddy. My stepgrandmother Bernie. Scott's uncle. And then Daddy. Even years later, his death makes me so angry. Daddy was a cool, smooth pescatarian runner, a nondrinker and nonsmoker whose health was a personal point of pride for him. And then he got cancer and died at sixty-four anyway. It's a cruel-ass joke, but he refused to feel sorry for himself. He fought that thing until the very end. He insisted on continuing his very painful dialysis if it would keep him alive long enough to meet his grandson.

Oh, yeah. My sister was pregnant. I wished I were too, but I was never really angry about it. The more obvious it became that Daddy was going to die, the more important it was to me that this man, who really wanted a grandchild, got one. He and I had a whole conversation about it. He was propped up in the den in their house in Little Rock, in a hospital bed, because he couldn't get upstairs to his room. So I set myself up in there with him.

This was on what turned out to be the last night I would

ever sit with him, after he checked himself out of hospice to hang out in his own house, the day after my nephew Alex was finally born. (He and Daddy got to meet a few weeks later, on Father's Day weekend. They sat the baby in his carrier at the foot of Daddy's hospital bed so he could see this grandson he'd stayed alive for. Two days later, my dad lost consciousness and never woke up again. We have a family flair for the dramatic.)

Before I went up to bed that last night, we had a Motown dance party, me twirling around his hospital bed as he sang "Please Mr. Postman," and, damn it, it was beautiful. I said, "Listen, this moment is not about me," to which he laughed, because I like when things are about me, and it didn't stop being true or funny just because he was dying. "Anyway," I said, pleased that he could still laugh at a time like this, "I want you to know that Scott and I have begun looking into adoption." Neither of us wanted to acknowledge the *And you won't ever meet this kid* part, but it hung in the air, harsh and unblinking.

"Don't worry about that," Daddy said, acknowledging it anyway. "Don't rush it. Give it time. It will happen when it's supposed to happen."

After Daddy died, Scott and I cried and clung to each other, reflecting on the absolute shitshow that the last two years had been. It was decided, without much discussion, that we were not going to be doing any more fertility testing, no more peeing in cups or bracing for needles or any of that. We were now forty-one and forty-two, respectively, and our reproductive parts were Dead Sea Scrolls–ancient, medically speaking. We could have spent time, money, and pieces of our ever-shattering hearts on doing more, but we wanted to be parents *now.* So about two and a half years after we got married, Scott and I went to our first adoption information session.

Movies do a good job of explaining, in a superficial way, how grueling the adoption process can be. There's much slow-motion crying and hand-wringing and then lots of "I just looked at him and *knew* he was my son!" while emotionally manipulative piano music plays in the background. What you don't see is the waiting, which, as Tom Petty said, is the hardest part. No two adoptions are the same, but every adoptive parent I've ever met has mentioned the soul-stabbing nature of waiting and uncertainty as well as the wall of paperwork. We were constantly churning through some intrusive form and then being handed another one that looked just like it but in a different font.

Then there were the court hearings, the ones that determine how fast you get that delicious-smelling baby or toddler whose little yearning eyes you can't stop thinking about into your arms, after which you'll immediately start dreading the moment when you'll have to let him go. The more time passed, the more anxious Scott got. "Are we close?" he'd say. There are so many rules about the privacy of foster children who are not legally yours yet. You can't publicly post photos of their faces or use their names in print. Once Brooks came to live with us, we were paranoid about breaking any of those rules, even accidentally. Scott was eager to be fully Brooks's dad, to be able to post photos on Facebook of this person he loved more than life, but for now we couldn't. We weren't even allowed to say his name was Brooks; we had to call him "Baby Z." I was so paranoid that I agonized over what name to put on the baby's turtle-shaped first-birthday cake, worried that someone might see the photo on my Facebook page and repost it. Not losing my baby over a turtle cake.

A little while after my dad died, we'd visited the very nice office of a good adoption lawyer our friends referred us to. We knew instantly that we were probably not going to be able to afford a private adoption, which starts at around twenty thousand dollars and can go as high as fifty thousand or more for a healthy white infant.

"Well, we don't need one of those," Scott explained.

It sounded better coming from him; I might've sounded racist about white babies. "I mean, we don't need the kid to be white. And we don't need an infant."

For my part, I never really got over the price differential. White people adopt more, so white babies are at a premium, and older kids or nonwhite ones are less expensive.

"You mean the black babies are on discount?" I said, horrified. If someone had given me a white baby, I would have loved him or her, even though I'd face a lifetime of explaining that I was not the nanny. Honestly, I had to have the conversation with strangers about Brooks, who looks like me, because people couldn't wrap their heads around interracial marriage, so they saw Scott and thought, *This white man must be the adoptive father, and this black woman who looks just like the baby is the nanny.*

Around this time, I met a prosecutor in the Family Services space who suggested that Scott and I become foster parents, which we weren't interested in. If foster care works the way it's supposed to, these kids' birth families get themselves together and they all go home together. After so much loss, we didn't think we had it in us. I could not lose anyone else I loved. I felt it would literally kill me. I turned out to be stronger than I thought, but that's never a thing you want to have to test.

We wound up enrolling in classes for parents who want to adopt *from* foster care. The birth parents of these kids have already had their parental rights severed, so most of the kids available for adoption aren't babies. Some are as old as eighteen. We were open to any child, but realistically, we were looking at a three- or four-year-old at the youngest or maybe a sibling group of younger kids. We were told that as rookie parents, we were not really going to be good for older kids or those with severe mental or emotional issues. We didn't know what the hell we were doing and those kids deserved someone who did.

When we told people what we were planning, a lot of them tried to tell us what a wonderful thing we were doing for our future kid, but we wouldn't even let them finish the sentence. This was not altruism. We wanted a child. We wanted to be a family. Good for everyone involved.

Adoption through the state doesn't really cost anything because the classes are free and we just had to cover things like fingerprinting. So, while it wasn't much of a financial hardship, it was a significant time commitment. That's an understatement. Watching two weeks of the Olympics is a time commitment. These classes were a second job, three hours each Tuesday for about ten weeks, and both of us had to go. Then there was homework, things you had to read every week, like stats on the types of kids that were available and how to not mess them up any further.

I think the classes are designed to be both exhaustively informative and an exhausting deterrent—that's really fair. The kids in question have been through it, and their would-be parents need to know that this is not a soft-focus Lifetime movie; it's a Netflix documentary. Remember the mythical white infants that people are willing to pay Tesla-type money to adopt? You will not find them in these classes.

There are well-meaning couples who come to these classes, like they came to ours, hoping that they'll be the lucky ones, the ones who will be there at the right time and place when that unicorn white healthy infant is available and just waiting to be loved. But that didn't happen with the families in our class, and most likely it's not going to happen in any classes you might go to. Most infants in foster care don't stay in foster care; they wind up going back to their birth families, either their parents or other relatives.

The classes we took centered a lot on the types of kids we might encounter, and the part that resonated with us were visits from parents who had already adopted and who spoke about their experiences. There was a *Scared Straight* element to it, and since I believe in real talk, it was appreciated. These kids are often fragile, disappointed, and fresh out of hope. The kids that are available have pasts and probably scars, visible and otherwise. They might need a lifetime of therapy and assurances that they are wanted and worthy of being loved. I think the state just wants potential parents to realize that these kids are not blank slates and that the goal is not only to help them but also not to do any more damage.

All of that made Scott and me even more committed to adoption and convinced that no matter how long we had to wait, it was, as he said in Yiddish, *bashert,* "meant to be." We really believed that.

"Our kid is out there," Scott used to say on nights when we were both hungry and tired and had almost fallen asleep in the Tuesday-night class. More than once. Anyone who's ever struggled to be a parent, by whatever means, knows there are times when you have to convince yourself that there is a child waiting somewhere for you. Sometimes you really do feel cursed. But then we would sleep on it and the next Tuesday would come around and we would say, "Eff it. We're going back," and we did.

At least one of the families that came to scare us straight was composed of white parents and an adopted black child.

We were constantly reminded that the majority of the kids up for adoption from foster care were black or Latino, while the prospective parents often were not. The frequent "What would you do?" scenarios we were quizzed on usually assumed the parents were going to be raising a child of a different culture and so needed to be prepared for everything from encountering racism to what the heck to do with that Afro.

Being an interracial couple very familiar with Afros, Scott and I figured we already had an advantage. I know that this makes it sound like an adoption competition, and that is gross. But the reality was that if there was a little black kid available, we thought that maybe we'd be a better fit than a family who didn't know anything about that experience.

"Hope I don't throw the averages off," Scott would say.

Being married to a black woman didn't mean that he was automatically equipped to raise a black child or even that he wasn't racist. (Yes, there are plenty of racists who date, marry, and adopt people of different races. It doesn't make sense, but neither does racism.) He was very honest about things he didn't understand, but one thing he was clear on was that sometimes the answer to "What would you do?" was basically "Who we gotta fight?"

During one particular exercise, we were asked to imagine adopting a child of a different race who was also a different race than most of the people living in our neighborhood. "What if," the social worker leading the class asked, "one of your neighbors verbally assaulted your new child and called him or her racist names? What might be the best solution to this problem? Anyone? Anyone? Oh, fine. Apparently Scott, who is waving his arm like he's flagging an Uber in the rain and whose wife is trying to step on his foot, has a suggestion?"

"Well, first of all, I'd go down there and find out who was harassing my child. And then I would explain to the person that they were going to stop talking to my child that way or there were going to be problems, so it was in their best interest to back up off my family. Is that the right answer?"

"Not really," the social worker said, sighing and also smiling because she really liked Scott, even when his opinions were not in keeping with the official teachings. "Is there some other way you might suggest dealing with the problem?"

"All I know," Scott said, "is that if that dude kept saying stuff to my kid, we would have a problem."

Fortunately, the social worker took Scott's stories in the passionate spirit in which they were meant and not as suggestions that he was going to beat people up. Near the end of the course, we had our first home study, which is exactly what it sounds like: People come over and study your home. They also forensically go through your life, references, records—everything. It was stressful. I took the day off to prep our house and hide our cat, Frances "Baby" Houseman Streeter-Zervitz, who, true to her name, would not be put in a corner. She was also not particularly friendly and did not deign to spend time with people she considered beneath her. Which is to say, she was a cat.

Scott went off to buy some fancy cheese, which the ladies who came over politely refused. They walked around our old condo in the old building in the not-great part of town, and I started to wonder if perhaps we should have pretended to live at the Four Seasons.

"There are parents," one social worker had said, "who keep good homes in every place you can imagine. This is okay."

Thankfully, our apartment was approved, and we had all this good cheese to eat, so it was a success. We were one step closer to being matched with a kid, we hoped. We had been talking about moving but were trying to wait so we wouldn't have to do the home check again. But when the perfect place came on the market, we couldn't pass it up.

We moved into our cute little green house, a little over two miles away, in July 2013. As soon as we were settled, we were going to call and get that new home study going. We were expecting more paperwork, more waiting, more uncertainty, and then eventually a call that we were getting matched with our child. That isn't the call we got.

About a month or so after we moved to our little green house, my phone rang as I was on my way into a Weight Watchers meeting in the newsroom cafeteria where I was probably just going to find out I was still overweight. On the other end of the phone was a relative of ours who'd been following our adoption attempts closely. "Hey," they said. "What are you doing right now?"

"I'm headed into a Weight Watchers meeting where I will probably find out that I'm still overweight," I said, hoping that no one was dead but that they were calling with some other momentous news that might keep me off that scale.

"Sit down. Are you sitting down?"

"I am now," I said, suddenly nervous about this phone call. But it wasn't that kind of call. Apparently, there was a brand-new baby in our family, one we'd known was coming but not so soon. It looked like his birth parents weren't going to be able to care for him immediately, and he needed somewhere to go when he got out of the hospital.

"What do you want to do about it?" my relative asked.

I had been talking to this relative a little over the summer about our adoption possibilities, and here was one we hadn't considered: a two-day-old little boy. I stopped for a minute and then realized that today, the day of this phone call, was my daddy's birthday.

"Maybe that's a sign," I whispered. "Do you think this could be a sign?"

"It might be," my relative said. Of course, signs don't give you babies, so they also passed on the number of a social worker who would supply us with more details. Before I called her, I had to call Scott, who didn't usually answer his work phone during the day, and he didn't this day either. I tried his cell. Nope. Called his desk again. Zippo. After a few more tries I called the main office number, choking down a slow creep of panic, like they were gonna give the baby away within the next five minutes if he didn't answer this phone *right now*.

"I know Scott's busy," I told the receptionist, "but I *really* need you to get him." When he finally got on, he sounded vaguely pissed, and I experienced a feeling of unholy wife smugness, knowing that he was about to shut his face. Yes, it was petty. I apologize for nothing.

"The baby in the family that was coming? He's here, and

he might need a home soon, at least for a little while," I said breathlessly. "What do you want to do?"

Scott's voice came back clear, strong, and without hesitation. "Anything we have to."

The next few days were a blur of interstate calls and me having to constantly remind myself that this might not turn out to be one more thing yanked out from under us. We were invited to take part in a conference call to talk about the baby. All I knew was that he was healthy but was unable to leave the hospital with his birth parents. There was a chance he might be reunited with them later. But for the moment, he needed somewhere to go, and the state wanted him to go to family if possible.

"Can we come get him now?" I asked. Of course it wasn't going to be that easy, because nothing ever is. Since we weren't there in Maryland, we could not, in fact, just come get him, because two states were involved, and we now had to deal with something called the interstate compact, which my mother referred to as the Magna Carta, although it was probably more complicated.

The baby went home with another foster family in Maryland the next day, and there he'd remain until either his birth parents figured things out or we were able to. Remember how we'd avoided being foster parents because of the risk of loving a child we couldn't keep? If we were going to do this, we were now going to have to be foster parents and risk loving a child we couldn't keep! Surprise!

Later that afternoon, a social worker dropped off a thick packet of papers, equally as thick as the packet of papers we'd already signed to try to adopt, but different. We dove back in and set up a visit to meet the baby in Maryland in about three weeks, which to me felt like eight years. But they sent us a picture, and there he was, this little boy that could one day be our little boy. He had wavy dark hair, tan skin, and a funny, off-center smile. That smile cracked me up, even as my heart was so full it was about to overflow, because I instantly knew this kid, and he was a goofball.

He was *my* goofball. Not officially, of course. Not yet. And, again, the point of foster care is to allow time for things to improve enough with the birth family that the child can return to them. But he was my family already, and my heart had already cosigned this. We even started thinking of names for him, this baby whom we hadn't met yet. At first, we decided on Max Edward, for Scott's grandfather and my dad, respectively. But that changed the day we met Maybe-Max. I remember them putting him into my arms, and I may have blacked out. It was all so overwhelming. He smelled delicious, like cleanliness and baby soap and happiness. His little eyes were closed. The moment was tremendous to me. But he had barely been on this earth a month, so who knows what he understood? I wondered, when I held him, if I registered with him as someone special.

I wanted to be special.

"He doesn't seem like a Max, does he?" Scott asked later. "I think maybe he's a Brooks."

Brooks Robinson is a Baltimore Orioles legend, the greatest third baseman of all time and Scott's idol. Not only was he an unbelievable athlete, but he was also the charming and relatable face of tolerance in a confusing and gross time of segregation and hate that I'm afraid we're close to reliving. When teammate Frank Robinson, who was black, joined the team, Brooks, the unofficial leader of the team—and also a white guy—greeted him enthusiastically so that everyone knew he approved and that Frank wasn't to be messed with.

Scott loved that story and thought it was a metaphor for our little family, proof that love and respect crosses all racial and cultural barriers and that happiness can be found in the most amazing and unexpected places. It's a Baltimore love story, and so were we. So even though it wouldn't be official until after Scott was gone, our son who was not yet our son was, from then on, Brooks Robinson Streeter-Zervitz. Long may he reign.

Sometimes when I am putting Brooks to bed, and we spot one of Scott's jerseys or something that he gave him hanging in the closet, I hug that boy extra-tight and tell him this: "You might not remember this conversation, little boy, and I'm sorry that your daddy isn't here, but I need you to know that he was sure excited about being your daddy even before he met you. He felt he was put on this earth to be your daddy. And from the moment he knew about you, he told me to do anything I had to do to make sure you were ours."

I don't know what that means to Brooks. But to me, it's damn near everything.

9

To a Deluxe Apartment in the Sky

I recently had a conversation with someone who'd never been to a funeral. I was weirdly envious that they'd never lost anyone they were close enough to that they had to attend his or her funeral, and also a little sad that maybe they'd never had anyone close enough to mourn in that way. I've been going to funerals since I was tiny. These weren't enjoyable experiences, obviously, but just a part of life. You celebrate the dead with crying, prayers, and chicken.

My sister and cousins and I didn't marry till our thirties, so there weren't a lot of family weddings growing up. But we sure had a lot of funerals, so that's when we would see all the distant relatives, the ones who were definitely related to us in some way no one could actually pinpoint, but it was cool, because they were family. *That's your cousin. No, I don't know how. Just say hello and ask if he wants some cake.*

The first funeral I remember going to was my greatgranddaddy Hairston's, when I was about five, and from there it seemed there was at least one a year. We went to so many that they started to feel normal, a thing you had to do once in a while, like going to the dentist.

Unlike dentist visits, funerals, at least in the black Baptist world I grew up in, are a social occasion. Not a happy occasion, but one that feels like a reunion. As with any other reunion, you wonder what you weighed the last time you went compared to what you weigh now and hope that no one says anything about it. And you check to see if you have some good shoes, or maybe you buy some new ones, and you make sure to ask someone about So-and-So's marriage, because you've been hearing things.

It's all of this, with a coffin.

About 99 percent of the funerals I've attended in life are black Baptist funerals. Two were Jewish ones, for my mother-in-law, Sharon, and now for Scott. Sharon's was a traditional Jewish ceremony about twenty-four hours after she died. There was the shoveling of the dirt, the beautiful Hebrew prayers, and the folks sitting shivah. The only thing that made it somewhat untraditional, perhaps, was the black daughter-in-law who'd been in the family for only six months and had to keep asking people what was going on, making the rest of the family act as tour guides through their own grief.

I still feel slightly guilty about that, but it couldn't be helped. People were asking me what time the kaddish was happening and shoving plates of nova at me. I mean lox. It's lox, right? See? I was bad at this. I couldn't keep the names of the fish straight, I didn't really know what the kaddish was, and I felt like I was in the way, up here in the advanced Jewish grieving class when I still had the books for the 101 class unopened in my bag.

I was, in turn, the same sort of guide for Scott at the black funerals in my family. He was right there next to me at my father's and my grandfather's, plus he was there at all the wakes and viewings, which were the day before the funerals and transformed a simple act of mourning into a comfort-food festival. I guess that has some similarities to the Jewish tradition where there are shivah plates and seven days of mourning, whereas we have two days of intensely focused pain and chicken. My mom and I refer to it as the Chicken of Bereavement, where the healing power of poultry and heavily salted pig-accented greens salve the wounds of grief.

But back to the pain. If you have ever seen a sitcom or a movie about a black funeral where everyone is freaking the hell out and calling on the Lord and jumping in the grave as the casket is being lowered into the ground—well, that shit is real. I can't generalize the experiences of all black people and their mourning practices, and maybe my family's just incredibly melodramatic. My friend Tess, an Italian-American reporter who was raised Catholic, covered a black funeral once, and her first reaction was *Oh my God, did they just find out?* because the level of rawness was similar to what you might see in the ER the minute the person was pronounced dead.

Scott said that he got the emotion of my family funerals, but there were some aspects he didn't quite understand, like the open casket and the wake and the funeral being on separate days. "Why are you spreading it out?" he asked me.

"Y'all do this for seven days!"

"Seven days at home. Just one hour or so at the cemetery. You drag it out."

Yes! Yes, we do!

How can I both honor Scott's traditions and mourn him the way I want? The answer is a sort of hybrid. It isn't going to be within the usual twenty-four-hour period, because he can't be buried on the Sabbath and because we are waiting for out-of-town people. My friends recommend an incredible rabbi named Cookie who is cool with officiating at a service planned partially by a black Baptist with theatrical leanings.

We agree to do the service at the funeral home that's attached to the cemetery where we are burying him, the one with all the packages. I delegate various tasks to whoever wants to deal with them because I don't deal with anything. Everyone wants to be useful, so I'm just giving people what they want. We don't have much time, and I'm only tangentially lucid, but I ask around about how much is *too* much for a Jewish funeral. My family's mourning-related affairs are the perfect combination of sadness, reunion, and understated tasteful talent show. It's not that we go out of our way to make a production out of it. It's just that many of us happen to be really good singers, and our genuine expressions of love are best conveyed through song.

Not a single person turns me down when asked to participate. Lynne selects an Amy Grant song that speaks of victory over death but doesn't specifically mention Jesus so as not to insult the Jewish attendees and Scott. I've let everyone know that if I hear one note of "My Heart Will Go On," there will be a riot. From me.

It's been decided that I'm not going to speak, because I don't want to. I don't think anyone else wants me to either, because it could be tabloid-level messy. Scott probably would have enjoyed that. But he's not here to have an opinion. I do think he'd like something sassy, though. At my granddaddy's funeral there was a woman from the mime ministry—a thing neither of us had imagined existed before that moment—who brought everyone to tears with an interpretive dance to a sad hymn. I don't think Scott would be into the mime for his own funeral, but he wouldn't want to be ordinary.

I don't like people feeling sorry for me, but in this situation, it's inevitable. I'm the widow in the black dress stoically dabbing her tears, hoping not to brush my signature Ronnie Spector Egyptian liner into my eye. There is no hiding for me.

With so much momentous stuff going on, it's comforting to focus on the minutiae, like the funeral program or choosing what to wear. The latter task I entrust to several of my bossier friends. I try on everything in my closet for them, including the leopard dress I last wore to a Belmont Stakes party on Palm Beach. Scott liked it because it was curvy and fun with enough boob but not so much that he had to say, "Put your boobs away." And he used to say that sometimes. When I put it on, I can tell immediately that my girls are not feeling it. So what.

"Scott loved me in this dress," I say. Nobody's gonna screw with that.

I have a good argument going, but the boobs wind up being put away anyway and we start from scratch and go shopping. My friend Kim, who planned my wedding, made me prune the performers because it was, she said, "becoming a talent show," now takes over the wardrobe shopping. Even with all of the bossy people in my house, no one resists her, because Kim, an incredibly successful social media marketer, business coach, and author, carries herself in a way that makes everyone assume she's in charge. She's even buying the dress, and I don't protest, because she knows what she's doing. And free clothes rock.

We wind up at the Ann Taylor Loft outlet. My friend Brittney pulls all the dresses, and Nikki and Kim act as the Michael Kors and the Heidi Klum of this very special death episode of *Project Runway*. It's as hilarious as shopping for your husband's funeral can be.

The winner is an appropriate houndstooth dress, sleeveless and in a size I hate having to buy. But it's pretty and I don't have to pay for it. We then go to a shoe store, where the clerk asks if I'm interested in something sexy.

"Not for this occasion," Britt says as I try not to snort-laugh. I love my friends.

Besides my friends, one of the other things keeping me from being a train wreck is Brooks. His little face gives me life. But I can't help worrying about the adoption, because I can't help worrying about everything. I'm scared that if I look too unhinged, people might think I can't take care of him. I don't think there are people watching me from behind trees or anything, but we'll have at least one social worker visit between Scott dying and the funeral. Even after Scott's buried and everyone goes home, I'll still be a widow and I won't yet legally be Brooks's mother.

I'm still so torn about what Brooks knows and what's too much or not enough to tell him. He's no dummy—even at not quite two, he knows something's up. But I don't know what to say that's not going to be about my grief, that's not going to put it all on him and make it worse. How can it be worse? I don't know. And I don't want to find out.

A couple of days after Scott dies, I'm out on the driveway, answering phone calls because the reception inside our house is awful, when Nikki comes outside.

"You might want to think about what to tell Brooks," she says. "He just asked me, 'Where's Daddy?'"

"Oh no. What did you say?"

"I said, 'Let's go find Mommy!'"

This whole time I'm in constant touch with the social workers, all of them, from both states, because the process won't stop just because I'm mourning. One of the social workers from Maryland, a woman I've come to depend on, assures me that Scott's death won't affect my chances because single women, especially relatives, adopt all the time. And when our local social worker makes her scheduled visit, she doesn't even come in; she just has me bring the baby outside to take a photo of him, to prove he's okay, then hugs me quickly and leaves. They're all being so accommodating. It's not a promise. But it's nice.

I decide Brooks should be in day care every day leading up to the funeral because he has a routine and at least somebody should get to be normal. People have showed up for the funeral so fast and in such large numbers that I don't have any time to come up with an explanation for why they're all in the house. He's still looking for Scott, still craning his little neck around the corner, especially when he hears a male voice. And it's never the voice he wants. I know how you feel, kid.

The day Scott dies, my friend Shelli, whose son is in the same Baby School as Brooks, volunteers to pick him up when she gets her own kid and take him to her house. I take her up on it because I need some time to get myself together, whatever that can possibly mean, so I'm not messy and scary to him. Shelli even offers to keep him overnight, but I need that other part of me, the remaining third. It reminds me of this Hallmark sculpture Scott gave me of three figures—a mother, a father, and a baby—called *Then There Were Three.*

"First there was the Daddy," Scott would say every single morning to Brooks, tilting him in his arms toward the sculpture, "and he was one, and then there was the Mommy, and they were two, and now there's the baby, and now there are three."

And now there are two.

The day of the funeral finally arrives, against my wishes, but I obviously can't stop shit from happening. I find that Brooks has a bad cough.

"He should go to the doctor! So we don't have to go to the funeral, then!" I say brightly. That goes over about as well as you'd expect, so on this Sunday morning about three hours before the service, as everyone else is getting ready, my mom and I drive Brooks to the burbs for a walk-in visit.

"They aren't going to start the funeral without you," my mom says.

"Well, they could if they wanted to!"

"No such luck."

The doctor we see is not Brooks's usual one, but she smiles at me warmly. I wonder if she recognizes me from the newspaper. Or maybe she just sees another over-whelmed mother having to hold it together.

"Do you know how long this is going to take?" I say, maybe too abruptly.

"Do you have somewhere to be?" she asks, perhaps wondering what party I was trying to get to that's more pressing than my child's health.

Well, since you asked... "Yes," I say. "My husband's funeral."

That's an honest answer, but I will admit that, particu-larly when I think someone's being an ass, I make sure to drop facts like this. Where is this credit card payment? *Well, it's my husband's card, and he died, so...* The bill we got from the ER for that visit where he actually died? Well, that was a fun phone call. For me, at least.

This doctor, however, is trained to deal with distraught parents, so she squeezes my hand, asks if I am okay. You know, human things.

"What can I do to help?" I ask. It's still so hard to say "with his father's death." But she went to med school. She knows what I mean.

"Well, he's too young for therapy. He doesn't know what's happening. But you? *You* need therapy. You need to be healthy. If you're good, he'll be good."

I promise to look into that and then gather my kid, his meds, and my mom and get back on the road to do that thing I don't want to do. "So I really have to go?"

"Yes, you do," my mom says. "I had to go to your daddy's funeral and nobody let me go to Key West. You'll be fine."

This is not the first or last time during this whole grief thing that my mother is the subtle, strong voice of reason. She's been talking me off ledges my whole life. No one expected me to be standing perched on this particular one, but she's been there too, and she knows how to get me down.

We drive over to the cemetery and park on the side, next to a hearse.

"Do you think that's for us?" I whisper. Shit. This is real. *Real*-real.

My mom gets Brooks out of the car, and I hand him off to Alana and Joelle, who had been his babysitters since he was six months old, hoping that maybe being with them will make it all less weird for him. It kills me that Brooks had less than two years with Scott, the person whose world he'd come to define. My husband loved me fiercely but I say without reservation that he would have sacrificed me to a dragon in a heartbeat if doing so meant he got to save his boy. And I'm fine with that.

Whatever composure I have melts completely when I see my college roommates Patty and Anne across the lobby. Patty has the worst cry face. Beautiful girl, but crying grabs her whole face and squeezes it like a lemon. She sprints across the lobby and throws her arms around me and then I'm already emotionally spent, and we haven't even gotten inside the actual funeral yet. We just stand there and sob and hug and snot, and any thought I have about seeming serene and beatific is done. That's a stupid thing to have expected anyway.

The funeral director explains that it's customary for the widow to inspect the body to make sure that it's actually her husband. I wish there were someone to delegate this task to, but it's not negotiable. Scott's lying there in the austere wooden casket, eyes closed in his Brooks Robinson jersey and a nice pair of pants from a suit he loved. He'd be mad about me breaking up the suit, but he doesn't get a say. You die on me? I pick your outfit. The look is completed with his Ravens flip-flops. He looks good. He looks quiet.

He looks like he's not gonna wake up.

My sister and mommy and Scott's brother, Josh, are behind me, and I can tell that the funeral director is slightly taken aback. I'm told that at most Jewish funerals, only the widow or the parents of the deceased view the body. This is a massive departure from my tradition, where the body does at least two shows, the wake and then the funeral, open casket and all. If this were someone from my side of the family, the whole crew would be in here, filing past the casket and crying or putting baseball cards in Scott's hands or snapping photos. We all grieve in our own ways. My family's is just dramatic and full of flair.

I lean over and simply whisper, "Goodbye, Scotty," and the lid is closed. I'm not ready. I'm not ever gonna be ready. But this funeral is happening with or without me, so we might as well get started.

My aunt Debbie and uncle Lester, both Baptist pastors, tell beautiful stories about how chatty and lovely Scott was, that he never knew a stranger, and that he made everyone feel comfortable, as if that were his job. It feels good to know that even now, my family still gets Scotty. My sister's Amy Grant song, "Nothing Is Beyond You," is as moving and genuine as I'd imagined, although I have to look away, eyes full of water, when she hits the line "Death has lost its sting," because all I can think is *Has it? Has it, really?*

I look at my watch and know that we're getting to the end of the program, which is supposed to clock in at about thirty minutes so we can get to the graveside and burial. I'm not opposed to delaying that part, but if we can't stop it, we might as well get on with it.

Rabbi Cookie explains to all of us that the reason Jews shovel dirt on the casket of a loved one is that it is the final mitzvah, the thing that person cannot do for him- or herself. But the best mitzvah, if mitzvahs are things that we should be ranking, happens before we even leave the funeral home.

The rabbi calls Scott's cousin Kenny up to make some remarks, *remarks* being something I always thought were brief. Nobody told Kenny this.

"The first story I'm gonna tell," he starts.

"First?" I hiss, leaning over to my sister. "What, is he doing a bit?" *Au contraire.* What follows is not a bit—it's a roast. It's a *Gong Show* act. And it's exquisite. Kenny, who mentions that Scott's final gift to him was to die on his birthday, tells us about the cousin to whom he was basically a brother; he discusses his sports obsessions, his hilariously bad driving, the family tradition of trying to jinx each other's sports bets, and his devotion to his niece and nephews, two of whom are sitting protectively behind me.

"Well, that's nice," I say to Lynne, assuming we're done now. We are not. I look at Kenny. He fumbles with his phone, then raises it to the mic. "So, my first song..."

Oh, wow. I glance at Rabbi Cookie, who looks confused, and I have to smile. If Scott is watching this somewhere, he's surprised it's his family running out the funeral clock and not mine. The first song is that sad one from *The Fast and the Furious 87* or whatever that was, the one released after Paul Walker died. It starts "It's been a long day without you, my friend, and I'll tell you all about it when I see you again." I'm not in the place to wax philosophic about blissful future conversations with my husband, who should be laying out his clothes for his first day at work, not hanging out in the afterlife.

Both this song and "My Heart Will Go On" have been emphatically banned from this function because they're just too much. But this is Kenny's expression of grief and I can't very well rush him and stomp his phone till the music goes away.

When it's over, he says, "This is Scott's favorite, and I think you all know it," and he presses Play again. Nothing happens. *Oh no,* I think. *Oh no. This has to work.* Immediately I know this is Kenny's mitzvah. It is all of our mitzvahs for Scott, to make this funeral the showstopping, arm-waving encore of his life. None of us want to be here. But we have to be. This is the last thing we can do for Scott besides leave here and not completely screw up the lives we get to live and that he doesn't.

Kenny takes a breath and fumbles with the phone some more, and Rabbi Cookie assists. After a few moments, he tries again. And smiles. Okay.

"It's a sing-along!" he says. "Everybody, come on up! Leslie, Lynne, y'all know this one!

"We-el, we're moving on up . . . to the East Side . . . to a dee-luxe apartment in the sky-y-yy."

Ah, yeah.

And soon two hundred and fifty people of various races, faiths, ages, and familiarity with Scott's 1970s TV obsession rise to their feet and begin singing along with the theme of *The Jeffersons.* There is stomping. There is laughter. There is joy—big, giant-stadium Valhalla joy that cannot be contained. Nobody here wants to be celebrating *the end* of Scott's life. They are celebrating his *life,* period. His totality.

His awesomeness. And we wouldn't want to be anywhere else. I look over, around the beans-not-burning-on-the-grill part, and Rabbi Cookie is stomping along.

We end on a high note, having finally gotten a piece of the pie, and everyone is singing and cheering and I'm laughing so hard I can't separate the happy tears from the sad ones, so I take them all together and hope I don't drown in them. It seems like good practice.

10

The Life-Changing Magic of Sloppy, Grief-Based Housecleaning

After the funeral, the concerned herd that has been camped out at my house since Scott died immediately thins. I'm both sad and relieved to see them go. I dread the silence, the stillness, but I'm also eager to get everyone the hell out of my house. They mean well, but as the shock wears off, the congregation of sad people is making me sadder.

My mom stays with us for a week, then heads back to Little Rock to pack up her house so she can move down to be with us. She was already planning to move to Florida, to a fancy condo a mile away from us. But on the day of the Bad Thing, as my mother was holding my crumpled body upright in my living room, I realized I couldn't imagine standing up if she ever let go. "Don't move in down the street," I said before I knew what I was saying. "Move in with me."

She paused for just the slightest second. "I think we can work something out."

Even a week later, I don't realize the massive thing I'm asking her to do. My mother, still mourning my dad, had been packing up her world and heading to Florida to live her best widowed single life with all the hot old single guys. It was going to be bittersweet but wide open with possibilities. Now her sobbing, broken child has begged her to co-parent a toddler with her. And she said yes, because she is magic.

I feel it is extraordinary that everyday life goes on without my husband. The night of the funeral, when the house is quiet, the food's all put away, and I'm lying in bed trying not to think, it hits me that my only reward for being brave and stoic through the day's hard stuff is just more hard stuff. I do not get the thing I really want, which is to have my husband back. What's left is the rest of my life, which I'm assuming will be decades long. I have to get on with the business of trying to figure out what the hell that's supposed to look like without Scott.

And...the hell if I know.

The day after the funeral, Brooks is back in day care, still sometimes looking at me like he knows I'm not telling him something. Why is it so hard to say? I mean, I know why. The first time I tried to write about my dad after he died, my editor, Larry, sent my column back with a note that said *Can you get deeper? It's almost like you're trying to avoid really talking about his death.*

You think?

I feel like a liar contributing to the amount of future therapy that my child is going to require. A few days after the funeral, not long before she heads back to Arkansas to pack, my mom insists that we walk Brooks to day care, both as exercise and for a therapeutic task that gets me out of the house and out of the bourbon and cake. The bottoms of my feet feel heavy, like magnets are pulling them to the earth, and every step is a struggle to yank those magnets off the ground.

But I don't complain. I secretly know I need the exercise. The obscene amount of food around me and the fact that I am a big girl who likes to eat are catching up with me, and the weight starts slowly rolling on. The wine ain't helping either.

(At the time Scott died I was a hundred and ninety

pounds, which was about fifteen pounds heavier than I was the day we brought Brooks home a year and a half earlier and nearly twenty-five pounds heavier than I was when we got married. I would, before I finally slapped the spoon out of my own hand a few months later, get up to two hundred and ten pounds, bigger than I have ever been, and I was not happy about it. Then again, I was even unhappier that my husband was dead, so if I had to eat this plate of fried green tomatoes with the spicy creamy remoulade, I had to. Healing!)

After my mother leaves, a series of merciful friends trickle in over the next two weeks as a sort of human grief bridge, to check on me and make sure I haven't lost my mind, because that's what friends do. These visits, from my friend Beth, my college roommate Sonali, and my former newsroom friend and bridesmaid Nirvi, allow me to keep floating through the uncertainty of my new widow lifestyle. *New widow lifestyle* sounds like something you'd find products for on daytime TV, things like comfy tracksuits and compression socks.

These friends are close enough that they know when to give me space but also to gently pressure me to reintroduce myself to common social norms, like wearing a bra and leaving my house. During this time, thoughtful people are still sending and bringing over food, just at a slower clip. My brother-in-law Josh, who hangs around for a week, appreciates this because I, his host, am too sad to cook. My friend Libby still calls every day to see if there's new food, which gives her a reason to stop by and check in on me, and because who doesn't like free food? I will love her for this forever.

The final visitor is my friend Jason from York, Pennsylvania, who's my brother in the way that half the people I call my aunts and my uncles and my cousins are family without actually being related to me legally or biologically. They're people you would brush your teeth in front of. In your underwear.

Jason, or Jay, as we call him, was one of my co–baby fledgling reporters back in York in the early nineties. I thought he was cute, but it was never like that with us. We both remember a conversation we had in his Jeep about how we were friends but, like, *real* friends, not just the kind of friends you say you want to be when you don't want to sleep with someone. In the eight years we worked together, he became my confidant, my reporting partner, my wingman. Lynne and I sang a Dan Fogelberg song at his wedding, and when I got married, he was my bridesman, sporting a purple tie to match the ladies' gowns, although he'd offered to wear a dress if I wanted him to.

When I introduced Jay to Scott, he told Scott that he had been my first Jew and that he was entrusting me to him. He knew I could handle myself but he wanted Scott to know he was being watched. When Scott died, I guess Jay resumed the responsibility of being the Jewish guy that looked after me.

I think it was Lynne that called Jay the morning Scott died to tell him what happened, and he called me and said, "I'm coming down."

"You know you don't have to," I say.

"Shut up," he says, and it's the sweetest thing, because he's not walking on eggshells. It feels good and normal for him to tell me I'm being stupid and to just let someone love me, already.

When Jay gets off the plane a few days later and sees me standing at the end of the gateway like I'm about to topple over, he just opens his arms and gathers me into them at the exact moment that I'm about to disintegrate. And I just breathe. Have I been holding my breath this whole time? I just get to sink and not say anything. He holds me up and all I have to do is not knock us both over.

As we hang out that day, I start getting a little nervous about what to say when we pick Brooks up from day care, because I know he's still trying to figure out what's happened to Scott, and of course he's still thinking Scott's gonna come back in the house and throw him up in the air and watch *Sanford and Son* in the recliner with him. In the past week, I've managed to get as far in the conversation as "Daddy's not here." I don't add *right now* because that implies that he will be here again on this temporal plane at some point, and that's a lie. I don't know what's going to make sense to a not-quite-two-year-old. I can't even say the word *dead* at the moment, not even when I'm talking about my stupid phone. I've just been saying, "My phone...umm, my battery's drained."

I'm really worried that Brooks is going to confuse Jason for Scott. Jason doesn't look a thing like Scott, but he is a funny forty-something white Jewish guy, so my heart implodes like a collapsing star when Brooks comes to the door of the day care, sees a male figure standing by the car, and says, hopefully, "Daddy?"

Jason is magic, so he says, "Nope! Jason!" and swoops him up into his arms and starts to laugh. Laughter is Jason's love language, as some book I never finished from back in the day explained. (My love language is hugging, listening, and, if required, restorative gossip and cocktail-buying.)

Over the course of the four days Jay is with us, we spend a lot of time laughing, eating, and just being. Sometimes you just want to be. He plays a lot with Brooks and it reminds me that this little boy does not have a father anymore, that he is now being raised by a single mother. I can't believe that's what I am. I actually remember telling Jason about ten years ago that I wanted to be a parent no matter what but that I didn't want to do it by myself. My romantic prospects at that time were...suspect.

"You won't be alone," he told me then. "All of your friends and the people who love you—we're your people."

I appreciated that, but I'd waited until I had a partner before I became a parent on purpose, and now that's backfired on me too. Can't I have anything? I'm just trying to get through the day without sobbing and now I gotta figure out how to keep my kid off *Temptation Island* by myself? (Nobody wants to see her kid on *Temptation Island*.)

Grief, at least for me, is an eternal reminder that you cannot crawl out of your own skin. There is nowhere you can flee, nowhere you can hide, and nothing you can drink or eat that will make it not hurt, not if you want to be a fully functional human being. You can choose not to function, but I don't. I can't. I've fought too damn hard for this kid, for this job, for this life, to not hold it the hell together somehow.

Decisions are hard to parse right now, but during Jason's

visit, I do decide I need to get out of Florida for a little bit. In the movie version of this scenario, this is when Julia Roberts would blow all the life insurance money on a ticket to some azure-blue-seawater paradise where the only guy in the village who speaks English is obviously the love of her life. Because I am not Julia Roberts, and because toddlers make torrid affairs with fellow tourists on remote islands difficult, I escape to Little Rock, Arkansas, to see my mommy.

The flight's a blur except for the nice man in our row who sees that I'm clearly distraught and occupies the baby while I turn away so he can't see me cry. As soon as I see my mother's sweet smiling face just past the security gate at Little Rock's Bill and Hillary Clinton National Airport, I realize I've just barely been holding it together with brown liquor and trans fats. Now I'm with my mommy and I don't have to pretend anymore. I can feel my shoulders relax, like I'm being liquefied. And I know that even if I dissolve into a puddle on the floor, Tina Streeter will collect all the ooze and put it carefully in a mason jar, then wrap a bow around it.

She scoops my grieving body and my baby into her car and takes us home to her big Tudor house with a deck overlooking nearly an acre of backyard. I never spent that much time out there, and now that my mom is moving, the idea that I wasted something I never knew was precious makes me teary. Everything seems to make me teary these days.

The smallest things make me consider my mortality, and everyone else's too. I can't even see a butterfly without thinking about my long-ago visit to Fort Lauderdale's Butterfly World, where we were told that these lovely creatures had a very short life span. All of those butterflies are dead now, and the ones born today will be dead by the time I get back to Florida.

I'm so much fun today!

In the interest of making up for lost time, I find myself sitting on that deck a lot, looking far into the trees and trying to suck in their tranquility like a vampire. I search for all that peace you're supposed to find in the natural world so I can be one with the universe and whatever, because the *Law & Order* reruns aren't working. (I'm joking. *Law & Order* reruns *always* work.)

The house is full of moving boxes, and all of my mother's friends tell me how nice I am to come help her. But we all know that's not the real reason I'm wandering, shell-shocked, through her carpeted halls in my bare feet wondering if it's too late in the morning to look this bad. I feel guilty because my mom is packing this stuff, selling this house, uprooting her life for me. She was moving south anyway, but it was to have fun and live her life, not to save me. With everything she has survived, I feel like I'm just one more thing she has to worry about.

I'm not very productive on my little grief exile, which is the point of a grief exile, I guess. I spend a lot of time crying while watching Brooks nervously to make sure he doesn't toddle adorably down the stairs. I don't know that I'm useful in any way beyond just being his mommy and the most familiar person to him. But he's got my mom and other nice older ladies who come visit and want to love on him and hug him, and I assume they'll pick up the slack while I'm crying.

One of my mom's friends, the very organized and decisive Miss Johnnie, comes over to lead the packing efforts. My mom has to go to work, so it's just me and Brooks and Miss Johnnie, who is aware of my family's tendency to pack-rat. We sift through all the boxes trying to decide what to keep and what to throw into the tractor-trailer-size dumpster that my mom has rented, now sitting in her driveway.

Miss Johnnie may have hoped that I would go against type. Those hopes are dashed when she sees me lingering too long over each box like it might contain the Ark of the Covenant or clues to the whereabouts of Carmen Sandiego.

"Have they even opened that box since they lived here?" she asks. "It's still taped up. That means she doesn't need to. Toss it."

Whoa. Those words trigger something resolute and probably fruitless. I am a widow of, like, two weeks, and memories and keepsakes are all I've got. This very nice lady here trying to make me throw stuff away? I must stop her. Right now, if someone tried to throw away so much as Scott's last Snickers wrapper, I would fight them. I couldn't save Scott. I couldn't save my dad. But I can damn sure save my mom's meaningful stuff...whatever that is. I'm suddenly picking through my mother's belongings like an auditor.

"You were the wrong one to ask to do this," Miss Johnnie says, not unkindly. She's probably right.

I know Miss Johnnie is trying very hard to be understanding, but she has a job to do. She wants to be able to show my mother a clean garage by the time she comes back from work. I am trying to help, but it's a counterproductive, sad sort of help.

I find an old Christmas stocking with my mom's name in gold glitter glue-gunned on. "You can get a new one when you go to Florida to replace it," Miss Johnnie says, reaching for the stocking.

"You can't replace my childhood!" I yell, clutching it close,

and I instantly regret it—I am genetically programmed not to ever, *ever* yell at an older black woman, out of both respect and self-preservation. Plus, I know I sound stupid. It's just a stocking. But it's *my* stocking. My family stocking. My ancestral artisanal stocking, part of the heritage of a clan that is down two members in the past three years. I can't get those people back.

But you're not getting this stocking.

By the time Miss Johnnie leaves, there's definitely progress, but still too much stuff in the garage and too little in the dumpster. I retreat, exhausted, back to my room for my . . . I mean, for Brooks's nap.

Perhaps it's time for wine. There is none at the house when I get there, so I have to import it, which is a challenge. There is local wine sold in the supermarket around the corner, a place so unfancy that feta cheese is considered a specialty item. I try some of the Arkansas wine they carry, and while I cannot vouch for the whole state's wine industry, this stuff is not impressive. I drink it anyway. Somewhere in the midst of the second unsatisfying glass, I decide that if I need to drink this swill, I have a problem. I call my friend Jon, who suggests that I stop drinking for three days, and if I can do that with no symptoms or issues, then I probably don't have a problem.

I do, and I'm happy to report that I don't have a problem. Not with alcohol. I have a problem in that my husband is dead and I'm trying to figure out how long I can avoid dealing with that. I am a forty-four-year-old mother hiding out in my room in my parents' house, where I have some stuffed animals, a sleeping toddler, and a TV. I have not had a TV in my own bedroom for years, since Scott and I decided to leave that room for rest, sex, and Ravens jerseys.

But now that I am alone, sad, not resting, and definitely not having sex, I am loving the watching-TV-in-bed thing. It feels like I'm in a hotel, but one decorated with pictures of college-aged me with my pixie cut and my sideburns like T-Boz from TLC. As I burrow in and channel-surf, I happen upon a documentary Scott would have loved, about Lance Armstrong and his fine sociopathic ass.

During my relationship with Scott, I came to realize that he hadn't always felt like he had something that was his. Sports were his one thing, and he wanted everyone to let him have it. But when you've voluntarily offered to share your life with another person, you have to accept that you can no longer choose to spend all of your money on Ravens memorabilia. Hands down, our worst fight was on one Black Friday in the middle of a suburban Baltimore sports store because he insisted on buying a pair of stupid sixty-five-dollar Nike Ravens shorts that put us way over our vacation spending budget just a day into our holiday trip. To me it was just a pair of shorts, but to Scott it was his autonomy, his individuality. He bought the shorts. We didn't speak all the way back to my sister's house.

Eventually even Scott had to admit that he wasn't going to implode if he missed a game or a jersey sale. I appreciated his fandom and what it meant to him, but it's not like the Ravens needed him to go in as defensive end or anything. "Who gets married during football season?" he groused to me once when a friend's wedding weekend coincided with a game the Ravens were just going to lose anyway.

"Humans," I said, hoping he wouldn't notice me rolling my eyes because the Ravens were choking mightily and it was the wrong time to pick this particular fight. From the outside, Scott might have seemed just like some sports meathead. But he was more than just stats and figures. He knew a whole year's worth of in-depth *Sports Illustrated* investigations about the most fascinating things, like conspiracy theories and details about segregation and how world wars and Prohibition affected the game, whatever that game was. He was smart, and that was super-hot.

So I know he'd have been absolutely giddy about this Lance Armstrong documentary. I hungrily gobble up every shocking detail about Lance, learning about all the things he injected into his body to give him an edge, and the way that he got the members of his racing team to use them too because there was So. Much. Money. And then he got everyone around him, sponsors and doctors and anyone who thought they could steal some of his shine, to cover for him. Everyone outside of the circle thought Lance was this brave superman who did everything he could to save the world. If you narc'd on him, he would ruin you.

And then he'd go hug a cancer patient.

Clearly this man was evil. And he almost got away with it too, like a *Scooby-Doo* villain. Because I'm in a very self-reflective place and because of my tendency to make things about me, I start to worry about Brooks. Grief and cheap Arkansas wine can mess with your head. I know that this is a function of my grief, but I can't stop thinking about Lance Armstrong being raised by a single mother, like Brooks will be. Brooks no longer has a dad, a male role model for being a good man and not a cartoon villain.

I know that I can teach Brooks how to be good and that most boys raised by single moms do not end up as sociopaths. Lance Armstrong was probably going to be a rotten person no matter who raised him, but I'm sure his mother didn't know what was lurking under that beatific smile either. I think about what everyone must have missed. His mom seemed real nice, and Lance was her whole world, just like Brooks is my whole world. My son is beautiful and charming, just like Lance was. Sometimes when someone tells me how gorgeous or funny Brooks is, I say, "He's also very kind and tells his mommy he loves her and remembers when he wakes up that he forgot to put his toys away. Tell him he's smart. Tell him he's nice."

I just don't want him to be an asshole. I don't want him to be Lance Armstrong. Perhaps that's a dumb thing to worry about. But worrying gives me something to do that doesn't involve crying or drinking. I'll take it.

II

Life Is Unfair

I'm supposed to stay in Little Rock for a week, then go back to Florida, with my mother planning to follow in two weeks, when she's all packed. At the funeral, my editor, Larry, told me not to even think about coming back to work for at least a month, and it's been a little more than that now. I'm not sure that I'm ready, but it's been decided, and not having to decide more things is a comfort. My brain is exhausted from thinking and worrying and crying, and the physical ritual of finding my work badge and sitting around people seems like the kind of drudgery I need.

But as the day of our flight home approaches, I can't bear the thought of leaving my mom just yet, of being alone without another adult to make sure I don't forget my kid in the Winn-Dixie. I don't feel competent to be in charge alone right now, and this makes me feel so guilty. After all, my mom's been trying to pack up her life, but instead she's had to rescue me. I still need her, and I think she needs me, too, or at least needs to feel like she's helping to keep me from completely falling apart. So she lets me crash for another week. We seem to need each other.

Maybe I'm not ready to be back at the house Scott and I shared. My friends have all asked whether I'm going to be able to sleep in the place where it happened. Some assume that I'm moving immediately. I don't know the permanent solution, but I do have to go back there at some point because all my stuff is there, and I don't have the kind of money that lets me just pack up and bounce.

"Do you think we should move?" I ask my mother, because I remember that, since she'll be living with me, we are a "we" now.

"I think you shouldn't make any decisions like that at the moment," she says (something that my therapist will tell me often later on until she goes out of network and I decide I'm healed enough).

I still don't want to leave my mom's yet. I don't know how I'll be able to stand all that quiet, because his ass was loud. I don't think I'll have the energy to do anything but be sad. But I'm running out of reasons to stay, because I don't actually live here and soon my mother won't either. So ready or not, Brooks and I fly back to Florida.

Libby picks us up from the airport, and the whole ride home I'm terrified of what's to come when we get to my driveway. I know I will unload the car, hug Libby, and open the door. And that Scott won't be there to greet us.

And I am going to lose it.

I feel like I've just been away from him on a short trip and now I'm coming home with so many stories to tell him. But the stories are mostly about what I've been doing to survive after he went and died on me, so obviously he's not here to hear them. I get out of the car and unlock the door, still hoping one last time that this has all been an elaborate, messed-up prank. I want to hear Scott's voice, see him coming around the corner in a Ravens jersey and boxer shorts. But I won't.

Scott is gone. This is our new life. And we are alone.

I want to hold Brooks as I try to get to sleep tonight, but he's tired and cranky and at least one of us deserves some real rest. So I put him in his crib, sing "Dream a Little

Dream" to him, and hope he can't hear my voice breaking. Then I get Scott's Ravens blanket and curl up on the couch, trying not to imagine him coming into the living room to ask me to come to bed.

I thought my mom would follow me to Florida in two weeks or so, but two weeks pass and she keeps calling to say something else has come up and it'll be a little longer. Every day she doesn't come, I feel a little sadder, a little more desperate, a little more alone.

One of those times that she calls me, Brooks and I are in an oceanfront suite at a Palm Beach hotel that Scott paid for, in a way; there was some life insurance money left after we paid for the funeral. It's Brooks's birthday and I'd asked him what he wanted to do. He'd only had one previous birthday, and he'd ended up covered in cake, which I wonder now if he remembers. The only thing I want to give him is his father back, but that's not on Amazon.

"The ocean," Brooks had said, and I turned around real quick so he couldn't see my face dissolving into powder. Right before Scott died—oh God, that's just a month ago—he started taking Brooks to the beach just so the baby could hear the waves, feel the sand on his fat little toes. Our very last staycation, two days before Scott left us, was to Fort Lauderdale Beach. We almost missed the cutoff for getting Brooks to day care on the morning we drove the forty-five minutes back to West Palm Beach because we were having so much fun hanging with him by the water.

Maybe he thought Scott was back on the beach? He wasn't. We could go look, though.

I'm just trying to make Brooks happy because it seems I've failed my husband by letting him die in front of me, so I'm overindulging my toddler. Right now I'm on the phone walking the halls of the fancy hotel's hospitality floor eating free bananas and pleading with my mom to join us.

"You're gonna miss the suite!" I say, and then I feel the sides of my mouth start to curl up because it's mighty hard to feel sorry for someone, sad widow or not, who's whining while eating free bananas by the ocean.

The truth is that as eager as I am for my mother to get here, I also know this living-together thing could be a hideous mistake. I'm a forty-four-year-old woman who for two decades hasn't lived in the same time zone as my parents, let alone the same house. I've done a good job of establishing myself as a grown-up, and I have a close and comfy relationship with my family while also remaining at a physical distance. I've kept my own counsel about how late I stay out, who I make out with, the source of that pounding headache, et cetera. My business has been my own.

Living with your mom erases that space. It's not like I have a porn stash or evidence of a massive bank scam on my hard drive, and I don't have dudes coming over in the middle of the night; I was married, like, last week. And my mother already knows about my wine. But I'm still nervous. Mothers have a way of looking at the stuff you do and seeing it as either a validation of how they raised you or a rejection.

When my family stopped eating red meat in the 1970s because my parents were concerned about the health implications, my grandmother took it as a critique of her child-rearing. "You ate meat and turned out okay," she told my father. When she tried to sneak me and my sister bacon or something and we narc'd on her, he gently told her that he wouldn't let us go over there unsupervised if she didn't stop. He was our father, and she was just going to have to trust his methods. I am the mother now, and everyone is going to have to do the same. Of course, I don't super-trust myself at the moment. But we're gonna go with it.

Before Mommy takes up residence with us, I have to conquer something else—finally going back to work. I do not want to, and Editor Larry reminds me that I do not have to come back before I'm ready. *So that'll be...never,* I think. But the word *never* does not appear on the due dates of any of my credit card bills, so the day after Labor Day, I drop Brooks off at day care and then drive my car, which I've never gotten the employee sticker for, into the guest parking lot at the newsroom building. No one's gonna tow me today, right? And if someone does, it's a sign that I'm not supposed to be here. Maybe I'm not, because my employee ID won't open the door.

Crap.

I try it again. No luck. People are starting to walk through the lobby and notice my desperation. They look at me like I'm a sad security risk. The reentry is not going well. Finally, the security guard with whom I usually discuss football and say things like "My husband thinks..." sees me.

"I'm so sorry," he says, rushing over and ushering me inside to the security desk, where various coworkers are now doing that thing where they pause, not sure if they should come over and hug me in consolation or just let me be. But me being back and not being able to get upstairs is attracting a little attention. The security guard swipes my badge a couple of times himself but it's still not working.

I suddenly wonder, irrationally, if I was fired while I was gone. Who would fire a widow while she's grieving? These aren't people who would do that. Then again, the way everything else in my life seems to be going, I honestly would not be surprised.

"This is a sign that I should just go home now," I say out loud, like that's not going to give this poor man another reason to wonder if I might be a danger to myself or others.

"No, no," he says. "Let me just call upstairs to make sure it's okay."

"Are you actually calling upstairs to see that I haven't been fired?" I say, aware that I sound a touch hysterical. Several touches. He smiles sympathetically and makes his call. I'm screwing up my plan to slink in, work quietly, then slink out in time to go home and cry before I have to pick up Brooks. That's today's schedule.

Eventually, someone upstairs assures the guard that I *haven't* been canned while on grief leave and that my badge has just been dormant too long and needs to be reset. He does that and then shoos me along to make my shaky way upstairs.

The elevator doors open on the second floor, and people there start to notice me. *Widow alert! She's back to halt all productivity with her galactic sadness!* Everyone is amazing, and sweet, and nervous for me. I'm so overwhelmed I want to collapse right here in the hallway. I hug my way to my cubicle and see lots of cards and some gift baskets sitting on my desk and around my chair. The grief equivalent of the Welcome Wagon must have been alerted that I was expected back today.

The first few hours are a blur of love and support. I peer over the cubicle wall and see an awkwardly formed receiving line taking shape. Some people come over to tell me how sorry they are; a few just smile at me, and one or two say, "You don't have to even talk about it. I just wanted to say welcome back." Those people are my favorites.

There's no real agenda for today and certainly no expectation that I'll produce anything besides snot bubbles and awkwardness. But I've decided to try to stick it out until after lunch. I make my way into my editor's office. He confirms that he doesn't really expect me to do anything today and that he wants me to take my time, and of course, if I need to flee, he's okay with it.

Oh, just one little thing, he tells me. You know That Girl, that column you have written for more than ten years, where you go around the county and eat and drink and write a story? Well, they've killed it in your absence because they no longer have the budget for it.

And, friends...I do not take that well.

I know that I am lucky to still have a full-time job in an

American newsroom, a job that entails doing pretty much what I want to do and not having to, say, cover municipal meetings or cops. That's someone else's dream, but it's not mine. (In the years after this conversation, I've gotten paid to sit onstage at a fundraiser, interview Pitbull, spend the evening at a Palm Beach resort in a suite that is larger than most of the places I have lived, and do karaoke with half of the Food Network lineup. My job is awesome.)

Things are changing in the industry. I know this. And yet, when he tells me what's up, I am not in a place to receive this news and process it in a mature and calm manner. So I raise my voice a little, then apologize profusely, mumble something about understanding and newspapers and thanks for letting me do such fun stuff and how I know we're gonna do other fun stuff and it'll be awesome. The hot-water spigot has been turned on around my eyes and I can't stop.

"I'm sorry," my editor is saying. He's a plainspoken dude and not normally an apologizer. "There was no good way to tell you this. I couldn't e-mail you while you were on bereavement leave..."

"I know, I know," I say, and I can tell that my attempt to make a low-key reentry into my place of employment is now blown. "It's just that I feel like everything is being taken away from me," I sputter and then I feel even crappier because I'm obviously talking about Scott, too, and it's not his fault he died.

A few days later, my editor will offer me an occasional Sunday column, which I'll accept. It's not a weekly subsidized happy hour, but it will look better on the bio when applying for awards, so I guess it's not a bad thing. But I don't know that in this moment, so I excuse myself and speed-walk to the bathroom, where I sob in the stall for what could be five minutes or half an hour. I try to cry with as little volume as possible, but it's a floor full of good reporters, so I assume that shit is all over the office before the stall locks. But they're also good people, so besides an occasional innocuous "Are you okay?," no one says a thing.

Remember our origin story, the one where we established who the hero (me) was before her all-important test? Scott's death was the test, the seismic event, but the tremors are the real bitch. They're lurking under the surface, these little rifts waiting to shift and crack and suck all of your resolve the way whole cars and luxury condo buildings get swallowed suddenly by sinkholes. You don't know when they're coming or how long they're going to last. The me before the earthquake thought she'd been through enough shakes to weather whatever else came her way. She thought she had this.

That me was an idiot. She didn't have an inkling what "this" was, what sort of life-demolishing force was hurtling her way. And now, hiding here in a stupid bathroom stall afraid of what people are saying about her, she knows— I know—there's no way to predict the tremors. The only thing I can do is ride them out.

I drag myself back into my editor's office to apologize one more time, and because he is a mensch, he pretends that there was no scene. And then I say, "So I think I'm gonna go home at some point soon. But not now." He nods, and I go sit in the cubicle for another forty-five minutes or so and then grab my crap and slink out on my own terms.

For the next few days, when I'm not making a mess of myself in front of people I can't bear to have feeling sorry for me, I'm holed up in my cubicle going through the e-mails that readers have sent me. During my bereavement leave, I'd been following the comments on the online stories about Scott and waiting for someone to say something really awful. Over my career from time to time, I've gotten crazy racist stuff in my in-box, and I'm bracing myself for the moment I find that my personal bereavement won't stop the usual trolls from trolling.

But so far, everyone has been truly wonderful, especially after I write my first column about Scott. In a weird way, it's easier to write than the one I did about my father, where I was hesitant to actually get into his death. The floodgates of pain have been dynamited open, and the words can't help but flow. I write that widowhood seems cruelly random, how I now had a lot in common with *Grey's Anatomy*'s Meredith Grey, a character I'd actually never liked until she was widowed at the end of the previous season, and how my friends and family—my village— had saved me.

A lot of the commenters are widows and widowers who share advice and stories and just a lot of heartfelt *I'm sorry*s. (This is two years before I get the *Well, that's what you get for marrying a white guy* messages. Assholes.) But I get one e-mail with the subject line *The same*, and for some reason I can pretty much tell what it's going to be about before I open it.

And...I'm right. Here is this woman, a divorced stranger, telling me that our situations are the same. In fact, hers is worse. I'm not here competing for a gold medal in the Misery Olympics, and I know that divorce is rough. I have many close friends who have been through it, divorces that in some cases were not their idea, and it is painful to watch them struggle to reconcile the ending of the love they assumed would last forever.

I understand the feeling that your life has been taken from you, and unlike my divorced friends and the writer of this e-mail, I don't have to avoid Facebook and Instagram for fear of seeing Scott's new twenty-four-year-old girlfriend. And I don't have to see him smiling and having the gall to look happy and not utterly destroyed.

My new pen pal writes that she's from New Jersey. She was happy, she thought, for a long time before her husband rolled up fifteen years ago and said, "I'm leaving you, my car is packed, nothing to do about it, later, tater"—and bounced.

Just like you, my marriage ended with no warning, she writes, and for a few lines she gives me some context—the difficulty of being dropped by your coupled-up friends when you're suddenly no longer part of a couple and the sudden suspicion that a now-single lady is no longer safe to let around one's husband. I get it. That would suck.

But then she keeps going.

In some ways, my situation is worse than yours—and now she's thrown her hat into the pain-competition ring. Even in my post-grief haze, I remind myself that I am just a face in the newspaper, not a real person, and that my story has triggered something that she needs to vent about. Even though she claims otherwise, she is not over this. She has not healed, because the healed don't pick fights with strangers about whose loss blows more.

But pick she does, and it's with an almost detached anthropological studiousness that I read and reread of how, after her divorce, her social group of married couples dropped her, leaving her with no support, an unfair and painful social isolation.

You write of your village, she says, *and I didn't have that. I didn't even get a party.*

Well then. It's right then that I decide to call her. She shouldn't have included her number if she didn't want me to, right? This is what I tell myself. I must explore this. Right?

Just tell me I'm right.

"Ma'am," I say after she picks up and we've dispensed with the pleasantries. "I'm not sure why, but it seems to offend you that I had the support of a village of friends and family and you did not. And I'm so, so sorry that you didn't and that your friends let you down. But it wasn't a party. It was a funeral."

She pauses, and I can tell she's not completely irrational, and it's probably unhinged of me to be calling her. My hinges are super-rusty at present. "So, here's the thing,"

I say to her. "I can tell by what you are saying that you have no interest in ever getting back together with your husband."

"Hell no, never."

"Okay. So, in that way, as a husband, he is dead to you. As far as his relationship with you and given the way he has described his relationship with your kids you have together, he is useless and might as well be dead."

"Correct."

"But your husband, as unlikely as it seems, has the opportunity to someday change and be a better ex-husband, a better father, even a better son or friend, depending on his personal situation."

"He won't."

"Ma'am, that's not what I am saying. I am saying that he is available to, should miracles happen, be those things one day. You are seeing him only in relation to yourself. My husband is actually dead. He cannot improve on his relationships with anyone, especially our son, because he is not just dead to them. He is *dead.*"

She hesitates, and I can tell that something I just said got her attention. A little bit. "Well, I guess I can see that," she says, and I can hear her bitterness starting to lift. But not completely. She is so coiled in her pain and this identity she's adopted as the Wronged Party that she can't abide someone else feeling bad, because then who is she? If she'd mess with a stranger about this, who knows how she's treated bereaved or suffering relatives or friends who didn't immediately consider her pain while feeling their own?

We hang up, and I'll probably never talk to her again, but I know what I'll say if I ever do: *Ma'am, if I didn't tell you last time, I am so sorry that this happened to you. I'm so sorry that you're hurt. I'm sorry if reading my story hurt you. And I hope that you are better and believe you can be better. We have to be better. It has to get better. Because if it doesn't, and five years from now I'm flinging my loneliness onto strangers whose only sin is not appearing to hurt as much as I think I do, I hope I'm rich and can just shut myself up on an island with a bunch of cats named after boy-band members.*

If it doesn't get better, guys, what's the point? There has to be a point, right?

...Right?

12

A Brand-New Life Around
the Bend

It's been two months since the funeral, and I'm doing okay, I think. I haven't fled to Mexico, gotten fired, or sold all of my child's clothing and toys so I can keep a twenty-something boy toy in luxury in a backyard tiki hut. That's an accomplishment. Still, people keep asking me if I've gone to therapy yet.

"Do I seem crazy to you?" I ask my mother, who has been living with me and Brooks, without incident, for about a week, probably silently evaluating me the whole time. She's a psych nurse, after all.

"Yes," she says. "But you always did. This is different, though."

In the Julia Roberts movie that is not my life, an overwhelming and catastrophic event becomes a catalyst for massive change. That would require more money, flexibility, and energy than is available to me at the moment. It's hard enough to summon the strength to put on shoes or clothing with buttons and zippers; a whole reinvention is beyond me. But I can start with one thing, and if that doesn't kill me, I can move on to something else.

I decide that that one thing will be therapy, because I remember what the pediatrician said the day of the funeral about Brooks being okay and able to cope if I am. The mental health of both of us is on me now. I'm sure that was in the parenting classes somewhere, but it seems like a hell of a lot of pressure.

It's been two months since Brooks has seen Scott, and he knows my mom, whom he calls Gigi, seems to be hanging out more than she ever did. He's such a happy kid, seemingly a healthy one, and I am still trying not to wreck that by saying the wrong thing at the wrong time or saying too much or not enough.

Right before my mother moved down, we were sitting

in the living room chilling, and he raised his little face, all smiles, and just asked me, "Where's Daddy?"

Two-year-old voices are cute and sweet, but his is the cutest and sweetest, and that direct-ass question posed in that voice sent me reeling. Did he suspect the answer? Had he specifically asked me while smiling adorably because he sensed drama and was trying to be easy on me? Or did he really want to yell, *Chick, where the hell you been hiding my father? I'ma report you!* Whatever he was trying to say, the moment had come. No more evading. I was not going to lie to my child, so I had to get this right. Right-ish.

"Well, honey," I said, squatting to eye level, "Daddy had to go away because he was sick, and we're not going to see him anymore here. But he loves you and he never would have left if he didn't have to, and he's watching over you."

I don't know how to explain permanence to a person whose footwear closes with Velcro. *But that's all I got right now, kid.*

"Does that make sense?" I asked, and he nodded, and what the hell was I talking about? He'd probably just nodded to get me to shut up so he could go back to *SpongeBob SquarePants.* I kept watching him for a few minutes to see if he seemed angry or damaged or was making a mental note to learn how to dial a phone so he could call Social Services to get him the hell out of here.

"Do you think what I said makes any sense to him?" I ask my mother now.

"As much sense as it can, probably," she answers, noting that I've been tap-dancing around the word *dead*. But I don't even know if Brooks knows what that means. I haven't even let him watch *The Lion King* yet because of the dead father part. I don't know if I'm doing this all wrong. I don't know anything. Which means I ought to find a therapist already.

I make a lot of unreturned phone calls to potential therapists that piss me off because if there's any population that deserves a call back, it's people looking for therapy. Then I come across a therapist named Sarah whose office is very close to my house. She is in my network, but still, it's pricey.

"Is there a better investment than your mental health?" asks my mother, a mental-health professional I should probably listen to.

"Hey, I have an idea. You're a social worker and a psych nurse. Why can't you be my therapist and I'll pay you in dinner?"

My mother smiles. "That's unethical. And you'll probably have stuff to say about me."

While I'm preparing to shell out money to make sure I stay this side of sane, I'm also spending money on clothes, but not anything cute that I want to wear. I now have a closet full of baggy, nondescript black shrouds, not because I am in mourning but because I am fat. And not just "I'm not a size 6" fat like they try to pull off on TV. Nope, I'm fatty-fat fat. And sad. There are plenty of well-adjusted women who love and honor their fat, who claim it. I am not well adjusted right now. I'm barely hanging the hell on. I wish I were happy with my weight because I would like to be happy with anything.

I've been a serial dieter since the first time jelly shoes were popular, since before jeans had stretch in them. Those were some dark days. Admitting my fatness is not about negating my worth. I've proved that worth just by still breathing and managing to get out of bed and contribute to society. But I am also eating and drinking my feelings, and the creep has begun creeping.

The middle-aged among you might know about the creep. Some people call it the mom creep. You gain baby weight and never lose it, and then you just start gaining a few pounds a year until suddenly you're thirty pounds heavier. I was never skinny except for that one moment in the early 2000s when I was following some crazy diet and working out obsessively. I got to be a size 6. I looked either great or sickly, depending on which old black relative of mine you ask. I was also apparently kinda bitchy.

"Size-six Leslie was mean," Melanie confessed much later.

"Size-six Leslie was *hungry*," I explained.

I maintained a comfortable hot size 10–ish for a while and then after marriage the weight kept on creeping. I gained weight after becoming a mother, even though I didn't give birth. In the months before we brought Brooks home, I had been eating clean and was faithfully making my own tomato sauces and green smoothies and cream of mushroom soup. I felt healthy and thinner and superior to all the sad serfs who buy Prego.

"You're not gonna be making fresh tomato sauce or coring apples once you have a child," my coworker Barbara told me shortly before we left for Maryland to get the baby. "You're not even going to have time to sleep or bathe."

I wish I had believed her. It wouldn't have changed the full-body tiredness that comes with motherhood, but at least I would have been prepared. Some women get back on their program immediately, so it's not impossible. It's just not possible for me. Right now I'm walking a lot with Brooks, back and forth to Baby School, a few miles at a time, so at least I'm trying to counteract the food. I like food.

Still the weight gain scares me, mostly because I don't want to die. I can't die. I know I'm not supposed to blame Scott for his death, especially because he had inherited some unhealthy genes and habits, but I have to be honest— he was overweight. He did not eat well. He worked out sometimes until he physically couldn't, and watching him in pain broke my heart. I always thought we had more time to fix it, but we didn't.

But I have time to fix *me*. I just don't know how to do it, and I have to figure that out, because I can't die on Brooks. I'm the only parent he has left that he knows, even if it's not yet legal. He has had so much loss in his life already—not just Scott but his birth parents and even the people who raised him for his first six months. I doubt he remembers those other people, but it doesn't mean that loss hasn't manifested itself somewhere in his little body in a way he doesn't even realize.

I cannot let my self-pity-wallowing, inactivity, and love of creamed spinach create a situation where I'm at risk of abandoning Brooks—or of being unable to lift him and play with him.

It's around this time that I get a message from Victor Ayala, who used to be my and Scott's physical trainer. I met him about ten years ago when he was the trainer for something called a Booty Camp, sponsored by a very glamorous friend.

I assumed Booty Camp would be some cutesy thing with mimosas and three-pound hand weights by a rooftop pool. But then there I was with a bunch of other women as this crazy dude made us do lunges around that tony rooftop pool or forced us to keep our backs flat on deck chairs while doing leg lifts in the hot noon Florida sun. And I learned there was nothing cutesy about either Booty Camp or Victor, who would make us all start over if anyone dropped her legs. We used to glare at each other like, *If you drop your legs, I will cut you.*

Victor was kinda scary. But he was real, and he didn't bullshit me. "You have the potential to do so much more than you're doing," he'd say.

"But I'm doing so much better than I was," I'd pout. And he'd just smile and throw a giant medicine ball at me. Dude was brutal. So of course I hired him as my personal trainer, and for years, off and on, he kicked my butt when needed. I was more dedicated at some times than others, but if I was committed, Victor always got me where I wanted to be.

For a long time, Scott's only interaction with Victor was when he dropped me off to work out. He hated working out for the usual reasons—it's hard and sweaty and painful—but his doctors, when I could get him to go see them, always suggested he exercise. He refused to join me at CrossFit or LA Fitness, but it occurred to me that Victor and Scotty were two of the most real people I had ever met, so maybe they were a fit.

Even though they were initially at cross-purposes—Victor's goal was to make Scott exercise, while Scott's goal in life was to never, ever do that—it worked. They got each other on a male level I will never quite understand. It's like how Scott could never understand how I could sit quietly in a room with my girlfriends and communicate an entire sitcom's worth of drama with a few sighs and Academy Award–worthy eyebrow acting. I would sometimes take Brooks in his stroller and watch Scott work out with Victor, hovering like an old soccer mom because Scott liked having us around. You can never discount the importance of someone wanting you around. And knowing that you're the person that another human being most wants around is some heady shit.

Also I could see how his body was changing, and it was hot. Scott was hot to me when he was heavy and his stomach was big, and he was hot when it was a little flatter. He felt sexier when he worked out, and we all know how sexy confidence is.

Scott and Victor didn't stay together long. Victor was moving around and then Scott got into a bad car accident that coincided with a rough, stressful stretch at work. Those two things made for a truly shitty period of Scott's life, even though he was happy with Brooks and me at home. There were times, I swear, that I wondered if it was going to kill him. And in a way, along with his not being hyperattentive to the things he knew were wrong with him, like the diabetes and possible heart disease, it did. This period made him weaker, made him more susceptible to the shit that was already in his body. The perfect storm that killed my husband.

So.

Asking Victor to work with me again now was, in a way, ripping off a cosmic Band-Aid, because he represented some of the things Scott tried to do in his life that did not work. It's pointless to dwell on this because I don't have any way to fix it now. It was all normal relationship shit—money, family, his sometimes maddening insistence on dropping everything when the Ravens were playing. I wish he were still here to fight about that stuff.

About two weeks after Scott's death, I get a Facebook message from Victor, who's been out of town.

What HAPPENED? is all it says. And I cry. I know that

Victor doesn't mean it this way, but it's hard to shake the idea that he'd left Scott in my care and that I'd fallen down on the job and somehow killed him myself.

I fill Victor in, assuring him that he'd done everything he could, because I know that Victor feels maybe like he let Scott down too. Not long after Scott's car accident, when he'd been unable to do the regular workouts, Victor called and asked Scott to work out with him, for free, just so he could see him. He could tell from his texts that Scott was stressed with his physical pain and the job. He was probably even stressed about how long the adoption process was taking. We drove downtown and the two of them just walked around the outdoor mall, slowly moving and talking about things men talk about.

"I don't know why I try sometimes," Scott said to me during that shitty time, "because it's gonna be shitty anyway."

He could be everyone's cheerleader, always upbeat, and then sometimes resolutely negative and full of doom. But he wasn't wrong.

My dad's favorite poem was "Invictus," the one that ends "I am the master of my fate; I am the captain of my soul." He recited it to me when I was maybe thirteen, and I remember thinking, *Man, that's cool. I wanna believe that,* so I did. But I haven't been feeling very masterful lately.

I'm obsessed with that idea that something bad is going to happen to me, too, and Brooks will be left alone. It's a scary thing to think, but it makes me want to call Victor. I may regret this.

A week later, at six thirty a.m., I find myself dragging my fat-ish ass up the side stairs at the outdoor mall by the Restoration Hardware. I'm ready to either cry or puke as Victor stands at the top of the stairs and barks at me like a seal trainer. Not a Navy SEAL. An actual seal. "You better get yourself up these stairs!"

Well, damn.

"Your husband died! You need to stay alive! You have a kid to think about! Don't you be feeling sorry for yourself right now! You're not some rich lady who has all this help! You have to take care of Brooks and your mom, and you owe it to Scott to stop whining and get the hell up these stairs!"

Did I mention Victor's a bit intense?

I need to hear this—I am here sweating and almost puking because I know I need this—but that doesn't make it easier. It's all on me. It always was, for most of my life, and when I married Scott I was comforted that I now had a copilot and it was never going to just be on me again. But here we are.

"You didn't die!" Victor screams at me with such rabid conviction that I am almost afraid to see his face close up. I don't want to see how angry he is. With life. With the two of us. With the fact that we couldn't save Scott.

It's so much harder to run or hit the treadmill than it used to be because I'm heavier, and that's just physics. It's all unbearable, that heaviness that's on your knees, on your joints, and on your soul, because it's more than just a physical weight. And believe me, there is a hell of a lot of physical weight.

It's *all* weight.

As Victor yells at me, he does more than get me to move faster. He moves something in my pride, and suddenly, as I lean against a wall, crumpled and sweating and broken, I see myself the way I guess anyone passing might. And that's not just because of the weight. It's because of Scott dying and that still-palpable grief manifesting itself as a cloud over my face. Now all of the work I've done on myself, all the races and the CrossFit and the stupid dieting, has been wrecked in grief and nachos.

And it makes me very, very angry.

Anyone who tells you that you are the same person before and after a trauma is lying to you. I am not the same person who woke up to make out with her husband on

July 29, 2015. I barely know who that person was. I used to trust people, to trust in my love for people and their love for me. But Scott loved me, and then he died, and now part of me believes that if anyone ever loves me again the way that Scott did, he is going to leave me. Not just reject me, but actually die on me. This person is going to lull me into loving him and then leave me forever. Which means I'd be absolutely no fun on Match.com right now.

I'm not Old Leslie. But whoever this New Leslie is, she keeps moving up the steps. I keep working. I am running—or trying to run—up these steps because I've got nowhere else to go.

And because I didn't die.

After just twenty (horrible, painful) minutes with Victor, I start to feel invincible. Not bulletproof or unable to bleed. Just not killable, at least not right now.

We eventually move the workouts to the downtown West Palm Beach waterfront, which is landscaped with a series of metal docks and boat ramps. Victor makes me shuffle up and down them holding a water jug above my head like a sad, flabby *Rocky* spinoff. As I try to figure out whether I'm out of his sight line so I can put the jug down without getting yelled at, I remember the period in my life when I was a badass. Not just in that Skinny Leslie phase,

186

but when I was waking up and running random 5Ks just because I could. I remember when I would look at an outfit and say, "I am gonna rock that thing."

I would walk into a room believing I was the baddest badass there. I was *Leslie Gray Streeter*. As I shuffle-crawl to the end of my workout—God, I hope it's the end—I remember that badass's confidence, remember her ease with her body, her ready smile. I remember her expectation that things would go well.

And then I know.

"I know," I say, gasping. "I know I'm not dead!"

"Say it again," Victor says, and he looms so large above the railing, it's as if he is the sun, shining on my weaknesses but also my strength. "Say it!"

"I'm not dead! I'm not dead!"

"Good," he says. "One more lap."

It's okay, though. I'm ready.

13

Healing: It's Like Putting Eyeliner on a Baby

As out of sorts as I am right now, I find it surprisingly easy to make decisions in extreme grief mode, because I have neither a filter nor the energy to muster diplomacy. I don't start cussing people out in the streets, but there's been a cord cut inside me that makes it impossible to, say, commit to being somewhere I don't want to be.

So after Scott dies, when people call to check in and suggest plans, I usually tell them they are welcome to come to my house. I don't want to wear shoes or a bra or have to care what my hair looks like. I don't want to go out and get the *Oh, poor widow lady* stares or hear one more "Aw, honey!" from someone with no way of knowing that each syllable of sympathy was an electric shock directly to my spine.

But now, a few months in, I'm venturing out more, and not just for work. I judge a cocktail competition for bartenders and don't cry once. And then Libby, who lives about a mile away, calls, asks if my mother is there with Brooks, and announces that she's on the way to my house in an Uber to take me to that social-drinking thing I've been pretending not to remember she invited me to.

"I look shitty. Go without me," I say, trying to avoid the mirror and acknowledging that I've turned into Florida's version of Miss Havisham but in my dead husband's faded Ravens jersey and tangentially clean yoga pants instead of a moldy wedding dress.

"Sorry. Already in the Uber. Can't stop the Uber."

I go because it's not the Uber driver's fault my friend is a pushy genius, and we wind up having a great time. Eventually I don't even need to be Uber-napped to leave the house. I meet some of my coworkers, past and present, at a happy hour, and when one of them says, "You get to not talk about it," I hug her really tight because that's just the thing I needed to hear. I just want to be.

But I have not yet road-tested my act, so I'm intrigued

when my friend Tess calls me and invites me to New York for Halloween.

"Just me?" I say.

"Of course not," she says, chuckling. "You better bring that baby."

I have loved New York ever since my family went to Radio City Music Hall to see the Rockettes when I was five. Lynne got temporarily lost following some lady who wasn't my mother out of the bathroom because she had the same purse, and little Leslie, compassionate soul, was sunk into her seat waiting for the premiere of *Pete's Dragon* to start and hoping nobody expected her to leave and go look for Lynne. *Y'all can find her. There's a flying dragon in this movie!*

The idea of a trip like this is thrilling but also terrifying, and not just because Brooks sometimes gets motion-sick. I'm scared that Tess will want to do stuff like talk to people and leave the house and I'm still not sure if I'm okay. I never know when I'm just going to suddenly need to curl up in bed and cry.

But Tess won't be micromanaging the trip, at least initially. She has to work a little while we're there, and so does her husband, Brett, so I have to entertain both myself and my son in a city I don't know very well. Even Carrie

Bradshaw couldn't do that. Not with a kid. She'd have left him in the Meatpacking District to go hunting for another pair of shoes she couldn't afford while wearing, like, a sequined toga and rhinestone Chuck Taylors.

"Do you think this is a good idea?" I ask my mother. "Can I still have fun? Am I still capable of fun?" I sound so pathetic, I want to step on my own foot.

"Of course," Mommy says. "And you will."

So I do it. I buy the tickets, take the time off, consult my therapist, and get Brooks a winter coat, since he hasn't experienced consistent cold since he came to live with us. A few days before we're scheduled to fly up, Tess tells me that she has been called to Baltimore on business for the day of our arrival, so she overnights me the key so Brooks and I can go straight to her Harlem apartment and chill for a couple of hours before she gets home.

"This is going to be fun," she insists, and these are nonrefundable tickets, so I guess I have to embrace it. Tess and I have been having fun for decades, since back when we did Indigo Girls covers at open-mic nights and drank too much Carlo Rossi jug wine, laughing till we fell asleep on the floor. She loved Scott—we actually had dinner with her in Fort Lauderdale, where she was at a conference, two days before he died—and she's doing her own grieving for him.

Tess is only a few years older than me, but she has always been my Italian big sister, the person who will rush me a glass of red wine if I look sad, then hug me and tell me what I'm doing wrong with my life.

I'm trying not to be nervous about the whole thing, but you should know by now that I worry in the absence of more concrete things to do, so I'm plenty nervous. I worry about the baby being sick on the plane, but he's fine. I worry about the Uber not pulling up close enough to the curb for me to manage the luggage, the baby, and the stroller, but the driver gets out and helps. I worry about getting me and the baby and the stroller and the luggage all the way down the street to Tess and Brett's building, but I take it slow and get there.

Turns out there *was* something to worry about that I didn't anticipate.

I assumed that Brett was going to be at his office, hence Tess sending us the key to let ourselves in. But he's actually working at home this morning. He's really happy to see us. And Brooks is happy to see him. He's quiet and beaming, staring up into Brett's face like he's the toy truck he forgot he lost.

Wait.

"Hey, Brooks," Brett says, giving him a high five. Brooks

stares back at him with a shy smile, and my hand flies up to cover my mouth. I can instantly see what's happening, and I know it's going to break my baby's heart all over again.

It's that Brett is a white guy with a bald head and square shoulders, like Scott. And Brooks has not seen anyone who looks like that since the night he went to bed and then woke up with Scott gone. He had the same look on his face when Jason and I picked him up from day care after the funeral, but Jay and Scott didn't actually look alike.

Scott and Brett do.

"Oh, shit," I say under my breath, quickly carrying Brooks down the hall to unpack our stuff. I want to explain to Brett why I'm shuttling the kid away, but I don't want to be a huge downer. In the three months since Scott died, I still haven't said the words *Daddy is dead* to Brooks, because what will that mean to him? Sarah the therapist says I need to tell him explicitly, in those words, so there is no question or vagueness about what I mean, that it's important for his understanding and for my processing. She swears that I'll find a way to when I'm ready. I think Sarah the therapist has a lot more faith in me than is warranted.

Brooks and I sit next to each other on the bed. He's wide-eyed with a rapturous look on his face.

Oh no.

"Where's Daddy?" he asks hopefully, and my heart begins to leak.

What I'm about to say could screw this child up for the rest of his life, could make his healing and relationship with death and acceptance easier or much, much worse. He's had so much change in his life, so much loss, and he's got to go through it and absorb it. I cannot protect him from this, and I guess our previous "Daddy had to leave" conversation wasn't effective, because maybe Brooks thinks he just left and came up to this nice apartment in Harlem. Maybe this is where Daddy's been all this time! Mystery solved!

"Oh, sweetie," I say, not wanting to ruin that beautiful expression but knowing that I have to, "that's Uncle Brett. That's not Daddy. He just looks like him. But that's not Daddy." Deep breath. "Daddy went away, remember?"

Even as I say that, I know it is not enough of an explanation, because if Daddy went away, couldn't this be where he went away to? Try again, Mommy.

"So that isn't Daddy. It's Uncle Brett. He's married to Aunt Tess. You know Aunt Tess? But that's not Daddy."

I'm talking too much and confusing Brooks. He looks disappointed. His smile is a little less bright, and the leak from my chest gets steadier. No, no, no. I'm supposed to be adding light to his eyes, not dimming it. I still don't know how to say the word *dead*. I still don't want to say it. But I have to say something.

"So that's not Daddy," I say one more time. "I know you miss Daddy, and I miss him so much too, but he's not coming back, sweetheart. He got sick and he's in Heaven and we're not going to see him again, not down here. I'm so sorry. That's Uncle Brett."

"Uncle Daddy?" he says, and I can tell that the little wheels in that tiny, beautiful head are spinning and that he is figuring out that the bald kind man down the hall is not *his* bald kind man. I'm sure I still didn't do that right. But he seems to get, at least, that this is serious. It's a weird moment. We surround kids in cotton bunting and cartoons about talking cars because childhood is supposed to be soft and fanciful. I've been trying to wrap this moment in softness and I don't know how to make it okay.

Later, I sneak down the hall and explain to Brett that whatever Brooks calls him, he's probably going to follow him around for the weekend, not because he thinks he's Scott but because he reminds him of someone he loves.

"Well, that's an honor," Brett says, reminding me of why I like him so much.

Later that night Tess comes home, and we have what

those of us who don't live in New York imagine is a normal Friday night for New Yorkers. Incredibly interesting people, including some writers and editors and poets and actors I know and others I don't, come over and drink wine and talk about politics and the upcoming New York Marathon. Everyone seems smarter in New York.

As I fall asleep, full of wine and friendship, it occurs to me that I have managed to keep up with my kid in the big city and maybe we had the first part of a conversation we'll be having for a long time about where Daddy is. He knows something's off, whatever that means to a two-year-old, and knowing that doesn't seem to have warped him too much. I hope we continue that trend.

The next day, the four of us go to brunch, and then we walk to a wig shop, where I try on a long brown one that will work very well with my costume for the party this evening; I'm going as Cookie from *Empire*.

"You're wearing this as a costume?" the lady in the wig store asks. "That looks good, girl! You should wear that all the time!"

I take my wig and go back to Tess's. The house party is hosted by a friend of Tess's from the ladies' rock choir she cofounded, and the choir will be singing tomorrow at a stop on the New York Marathon route. Brooks will be going as Prince, though of course he does not know who Prince is or even what Halloween is. Last year Scott and I put him in a Frankenstein costume, a vest, and a fedora and called him Frank N. Sinatra. We thought it was super-clever but the baby just looked annoyed. Someday he'll want to pick his own costumes and not be a living testament to his parents' coolness. But today is not that day, so I put conditioner in his hair to make it extra-wavy and then take great pleasure in putting him in the tiny blazer that my mom and I dyed purple. I also give him a thin Prince mustache, drawn on in eyeliner.

"Sorry, baby," I say, snapping a photo because he's so cute even when giving Mommy the baby side-eye. At the party, everyone coos over Brooks and wants to know more about me. Poor, unsuspecting party guests. I tell the story of my widowhood way too many times for me to be fun. (If you were at a Halloween party in the Bronx in 2015 where some sad lady in a wig holding a baby ruined your night with sob stories about her dead husband, I owe you a beer.)

Anyway, I suddenly feel depleted and not at all fun. But Tess makes me walk around and drink caffeine and smile at people. This is why she invited me and she isn't going to let me weasel out. Also she doesn't want to leave yet.

Brooks starts to fuss because he's a baby dressed as

Prince at a house party and he wants to go to sleep. The kind hostess sees me struggling and invites me to take Brooks into her room for a break. Oh, thank God. Eventually, Brooks passes out, and I put him on the floor surrounded by coats in the host's bedroom. And in about an hour, I pretend I'm going to check on him, but really I go to wrap myself around him, and I fall asleep right on the floor next to him. I know this must be strange for the guests who don't know me and just want to get their coats and go home.

The next morning, Tess wakes us up for coffee and tells us that she has to go to the marathon stop and sing with her badass ladies' rock choir but that she understands we're not ready to go with her yet. I love that she knows when I just want to be.

Brooks and I hang out in the apartment with Brett, who is watching football, and I get nervous again because this is a very Scott thing to do. Brooks might get confused. I know, I know. I can't shield him from this stuff. Brooks follows Brett down the hall and beams at him, but he doesn't call him Daddy again. Progress.

Not only do we not make it out to see Tess at her marathon stop, but we wind up missing our flight from LaGuardia because traffic is so bad after the marathon that we can't get out of the neighborhood. I talk with a very nice JetBlue agent who tries to find us a flight the next morning, but they're so expensive. The only thing to do, and it's still not cheap, is catch a different flight out of JFK, so we have to take an Uber across town, which costs more than a hundred bucks. I wish I could stay another night, but tomorrow everyone has to go back to work and no one is going to take me to brunch, so we might as well go home. Tess and Brett walk us out to the Uber, hug us really tight, and tell us to come back soon.

"I don't want you to go," Tess says, and I don't want to go either. New York is magic and has wigs and doughnuts and old black ladies on Lexington who yell at you that your baby's head is falling over in the stroller as he sleeps, scolding you like they are your grannies, and their nosiness makes me feel warm. I will take all of the aunties. All of the nosiness. I feel like I'm living. I'm here in the city and I'm still alive.

Brooks, who has been so sweet this whole trip, loses his damn mind on the plane back to Florida. It's late and traveling sucks, so this seems like a good time to poke Mommy with his little finger every time she starts to fall asleep or looks like she's enjoying this episode of *Blue Bloods*.

"Mom-*meeeeee!*" he trills, and I try not to look at the

other passengers, who are attempting to sleep and considering throwing their minibottles of Jack Daniel's at me. I want to say, *I'm so sorry, but he's two and processing his father's death after a long weekend of travel.*

Brooks passes out literally as we're landing, so I toss him in the stroller and head to the curb, where my mom is waiting like a benevolent spirit to whisk us into a car that I will not have to pay for.

"How did it go?" she asks.

"Good," I say. "I think it went good."

And then, even though the ride home is just ten minutes, I fall asleep. Your girl is exhausted. I have plans to make.

14

Will It Be "Yes" or Will It Be "Sorry"?

Fresh from my triumphant journey on which I managed not to leave my child in a bodega, the State of Maryland buys me another set of plane tickets. This time we're headed to the Baltimore County Circuit Court for the hearing in which Brooks's birth parents' rights may be terminated.

At this point, the birth parents have been served papers declaring the state's intention to terminate those rights, because the state believes that is what's best for Brooks. But anything could happen. The social workers have been very clear on the dangers of assuming anything, ever, until there are signed papers and official seals and such. All I know is that there will be a hearing, that the birth parents may or may not be there—they know about it but haven't said if they will be present—and that I'm going to have to gut through it no matter what.

Every day since I held him for the first time, two years ago, I have been falling in love with this little boy. As much as I have always known there was a possibility that he might not stay with us, even when he came to Florida, I have been falling, have fallen, am now incapable of getting up from this love. It has flattened me. And now that Scott is gone, I have to make this work, because I believe I am the best thing for Brooks, because he is the best thing for me. The only thing, sometimes, keeping me alive.

Scott and I did everything right, followed all the rules, did all of the things and showed all of the love, and now I have to do all the loving by myself. It's so funny that I insisted, back in my twenties, that I never wanted to be a single mother, and now here I am. And I am good at it, maybe because I have to be. I am Brooks's mother, the one he knows, and I am clinging to the hope that the court sees it that way. But nothing is legal yet and I'm scared that this won't go my way, because there's an established history of things not going my way.

But we're a team, me and him. I'm his mother, and he's my son. I don't know if he remembers his previous foster parents, because he hasn't seen them since he was six months old and now he's two. If you think explaining death to a toddler is a doozy, try explaining adoption, or court proceedings, or the possibility that he might have to go live with other people he doesn't know. It's not supposed to be about me. But I need him.

If Scott's death didn't kill me, I know that losing Brooks would. And I will do everything in my power to make sure that doesn't happen. I laugh now at how Scott and I used to complain about the frequency of the social worker visits or having to get the exact right kind of lock for the kitchen cabinet Brooks wasn't even able to open yet. Now, in this uncertainty, I would buy every lock ever made if that was going to guarantee him staying with me forever.

I can't help but feel for his birth parents, because I love them, and I know they love Brooks too. Again, I'm going to invoke the Tom Cruise Adoption Privacy clause and not spill a lot of other people's business that's not mine to share. But know that if some things were different, they would be raising him, and I would not be.

Since pretty much the minute Brooks came to us, the plan has been "reunification concurrent with adoption," which basically means that it could go either way. The state has to have a permanency plan because no one wants kids to be in foster care indefinitely. This does not mean that these plans happen fast—when Scott died, we'd been in the mix to raise and then adopt Brooks for almost two years, since he was two days old. That was September 2013. It's now November 2015. And it's still not over.

Technically my mother and I don't have to be at the hearing because we aren't official parties in this process. We're just working with the state, so we don't even get to speak. But I need to be here. Whatever happens, I need to be a witness to it.

"You might have to stop me from saying something," I tell my mother.

"I will literally step on your foot if you do," she says.

I ask Brooks's lawyer if they're going to mention Scott at all, and she tells me probably not. This guts me. He's supposed to be here with me, holding my hand and saying dumb stuff that might risk getting us kicked out of the courtroom but that will also make me snicker and calm the hell down. Scott wasn't just some guy. He's Brooks's dad, and the fact that he is not going to be here to raise him or even officially adopt him is a slap in the face.

I still can't get over the fact that, assuming we get

through this day and the parental rights are rescinded and Brooks becomes my son, he won't ever officially be Scott's. It feels like Scott's being erased. He's not even on the paperwork.

The lawyer and the social workers tell me that it's okay to have people there to support me but that they might not be able to come into the courtroom. They also say, again, that I probably won't be called to testify, because they think that the case is strong enough without me. They say they don't expect Brooks's birth parents to appear, but since the process has started, it has to play out with or without them. I have not seen them in person since the whole thing began, and as much as I love them and want them to be okay, I admit the idea of seeing them makes me nervous. What would I say? Will there be drama? I don't want drama. I just want to love my son and for the state to say that's who he is. And it's important that the birth parents know that I love him too, that my love for him is part of my love for them.

I fully want to say this to them one day. I just don't know if this is the day.

I am nauseated the morning of the hearing. I can't eat anything. And you know all about my affection for my current boyfriend, Food. I leave Brooks with Lynne at her place, about thirty minutes away from the courthouse, but as I'm heading out, he looks up from whatever he's playing with. "Where going, Mommy?" he asks.

"Gigi and I gotta do a thing," I say, rushing out the kitchen door. "Love you! K-thanks-bye!"

I annoy my mom with my back-seat driving and yelling at all of the cars that aren't moving the hell out of the way. "I don't want to mess this up," I say as we drive. I'm desperate for some control over this situation, *any* situation, but I know I have none. I can't do anything. At this point, it's all up to the judge and God. Hope at least one of them likes me.

We get to the courthouse and pull into the lot where Scott and I parked the day they let us take baby Brooks home for the first time. It had taken us six months to be able to do so, and we were grinning like jack-o'-lanterns. Brooks, who had just been removed from the arms of the only parents he'd known, looked less enthused. My inner drama queen is thinking about how gutting it would be to lose Brooks in the same place we got him.

Shut up, Leslie, I think. *Just shut up.*

I have always been a worrier disguised as an optimist. My mother says that even as a toddler, I often looked silently into space with a tiny furrowed brow as if I had the weight of the world on my little shoulders. I am a person who creates her own signs to portend the crappy things I believe are on their way, so I also need to recognize signs that good things might happen. Here are two—Melanie, waiting for me outside the courthouse and looking fabulous, and Jason, who has surprised me by driving down from Pennsylvania to hold my hand. I want to make some joke, as is our tradition, but instead I just hug him.

Entourage size is probably not on the judge's checklist of important items, but it can't hurt. When we finally find the courtroom, I see Brooks's lawyer and his social workers are waiting on the benches outside. Also waiting: Scott's best friend, Other Jason, plus my friend Rissa. Seeing all of these people here not only overwhelms me but also reinforces just how serious this day is. They're not missing work and reorganizing their schedules for something that has no weight.

It's *all* weight.

The sight of the lawyer representing Brooks's birth parents sets off a Rube Goldberg–esque machine of panic. It starts with a golf-ball-size thought in my nervous brain that's kicked off with an uncertain whisper and goes down a rickety chute toward my heart. They're not here, at least not yet, but I'm instantly scared. My mom sees that I am freaking out and squeezes my hand extra-hard.

The social workers explain that as wonderful as it is that my family and friends are here, only my mom can come into the courtroom with me. Apparently, the birth parents' attorney is very good and might use anything, including sudden outbursts of "What the hell, man?," to their advantage, to slow the process.

I feel untethered, but I can't be. I need to convince people that, no matter what, I am the steadiest rock in the world for this boy, especially since now I'm doing it without Scott.

But I'm not a rock. I'm a nervous forty-four-year-old widow who is living with her mother and missing her dead husband. The doors to the courtroom open, and my mom and I hold hands and walk inside, settling in the back. Every time the door opens behind me, I'm nervous that it's the birth parents or even some mystery person running in with last-minute papers to prove that I'm not fit to raise a child.

For what seems like an hour but probably isn't, Mommy and I sit in the courtroom. The judge seems cool and fair. There isn't even any testimony because Brooks's lawyer believes the case speaks for itself. I'm a person of a million words, so I'm kinda iffy on this idea that less is more. Then again, I'm not a lawyer, so I'm willing to concede, just this once, that I don't know everything.

The defense attorney does everything he can to cast doubt that the state's done enough to make this decision right now, and the state does everything to prove that it has. They go back and forth like in a tennis match, and whenever the defense attorney speaks, I sit up a little straighter and then notice that my mother's foot is right next to mine, and her heels look kinda high, like they'd hurt. I resist the urge to react any further.

Brooks's attorney refers to the baby's foster mother, and I gasp to myself, because it's just "foster mother," not "foster parents." It's not "this child also used to have a foster father who loved him more than the whole world."

"I feel like they're erasing Scott," I whisper to my mother. There's a reason there aren't a lot of photos of Brooks and me together for the first couple years of his life, and it's that Scott always had him in his arms. And now the official state narrative doesn't even mention him. I hate this so much.

Both sides rest, and the judge says she's going to take some time to review. "What do you think? Do you think it's going okay?" I ask my mother.

"I do," she says, the *but you never know* left mercifully unsaid.

As we wait outside with the rest of our tribe, Melanie takes a look into the courtroom through the door.

"Is that the judge?" she asks. I nod. "Good thing we didn't go in. I think I used to teach her son."

Whew! That could have been seen as a conflict, that my friend and the judge had a connection, however tenuous. Dodged that one. That seems like one more fortuitous thing to happen, and along with all the support from the people who've taken time from their lives to come sit in a courtroom to make sure I'm okay, it's another mitzvah. Yiddish has so many applications.

The judge sits back down and says she's made a decision. She then goes through every aspect of the cases presented by both sides. When she gets to the end of her detailed explanation of the thing that will determine my future happiness, she says what I've been waiting to hear: The state's motion is granted, and the decision is that the parental rights are severed.

Just like that.

"Did this just happen?" I ask my mother. It's so subtle that I feel like I must have missed something. Where is the dramatic gavel? Where is Olivia Benson to hug me and give me a pep talk about justice? Where is the loud *chun-chun!* sound from *Law & Order?*

We walk back out into the lobby, and the social workers come over to hug me. "So that's good, right?" I say, and they look at me like, *Girl, keep up!*

Yes, damn it, this is good! Of course, there is the thirty-day appeals period, but they think that the defense attorney is realistic and a good person. They believe he probably sees that drawing this out isn't going to make a difference. "So what happens now?" I ask.

They tell me that if the rescinding of the parental rights holds through the appeals period, the adoption could be finalized before the end of the year. Wait—it's November, and the year ends in a month. After all this time, after all this pain and all this nervousness, Brooks could legally be my son in a month. I have to fight back the urge to cry.

"It's okay to cry," one of the social workers says. "It's a big deal."

Having a big deal that's not about death or loss is so overwhelming, so different than what's happened in my life since July 29, that I can't even process it immediately. My luck is changing. Good things are happening. *It's okay to believe that, Leslie,* I tell myself, even though Leslie's been burned before and is suspicious of your bullshit.

I try my best to focus on what everyone is saying about the next steps. What's coming is more back-and-forth about paperwork. I'll have to renew my foster-care license. There will be more visits and probably new social workers. If all goes well, there will be an end date. Could be the end of the year. Could be the middle of next year. But it's probably going to happen.

"Well, kid," the lawyer says, "you've been waiting so long. What's a little more waiting? With everything you've been through."

And right now, ladies and gents, is when I stop whining, at least for the moment, and decide to take the good news and shut the hell up. I haven't felt this content, this light, in forever. I have earned this. My friend Libby always tells me that the universe owes us nothing, but I gotta say that right now, I feel I'm being rewarded for all of the crap I've gone through. The fried rice and cocktails we have later at the P. F. Chang's at the mall I used to work at are celebratory. They are my gift. The fried rice of hope. And it's delicious.

15

Ready to Take a Chance Again. Maybe. Probably.

I have a running list of the art that Scott has ruined for me by dying: movies I can't watch anymore, songs I rush to turn off during the opening chords, books on our bookshelf my eyes quickly skip over. The list includes previous favorite *Sleepless in Seattle* (Tom Hanks is widowed with a kid who is afraid of forgetting his mom), most Gloria Estefan ballads about not being able to live without one's beloved, *The Andy Griffith Show* (did Opie ever get therapy when his mom died?), and our wedding song, Stephen Bishop's "It Might Be You" from the movie *Tootsie*. We chose that because I'd found the answer.

There was no question. It was him. It was Scott. And now it's not. Stupid song.

Scott's death did give me new appreciation for a movie or two that I'd been "meh" on before. One was *Practical Magic,* where reluctant witch Sandra Bullock conjures up a man to beat a family curse that prohibits her from love and then collapses into guilty grief when he dies. She blames herself because she believes, even though they loved each other deeply and have two dear daughters, that maybe he died because she dragged him into a situation she created by trying to thwart her undeniable fate—to be alone forever. But all is not lost; she eventually finds love with hot Aidan Quinn, who knows about her weirdness and damage but also her magic and loves her for all of it. Her first husband and his loss will always be a part of her life, but that becomes part of the foundation for a second chance.

That didn't mean anything to twenty-eight-year-old single me. But it means a whole lot now.

The other one is *Must Love Dogs,* with John Cusack and Diane Lane as meet-cute forty-somethings whose conflicts and bumbles are just annoying stumbling blocks on the way to their inevitable reunion and happy-ever-after. Nobody comes to these sorts of movies for the pretty people not to end up together. It's a silly movie, but there's an interesting subplot involving Diane Lane's widowed father, played by Christopher Plummer, who's still super-smooth, and a quirky, many-times-divorced lady named Dolly, played by Stockard Channing.

Dolly falls helplessly in love with Christopher Plummer, because who wouldn't, since he's dapper and quotes Irish poets at family gatherings. She thinks that he might finally be that everlasting love that's always eluded her but then has her heart broken when Christopher Plummer invites two other women to Thanksgiving dinner. (That's shady. Use your words, Christopher Plummer, not multiple ambush dates.)

The first time I saw it, at thirty-four, I identified with Dolly, the lonely lady who thought she'd finally found the One, and I considered Christopher Plummer the villain here. But in my widowhood, I get him now. He appreciates the life he still has, and he doesn't want to be lonely. But he's not lying to anybody either—"I had the love of my life," he tells Diane Lane, and he means it.

At thirty-four I saw that as some sort of selfish, stubborn fear of opening himself up that would allow him to play the geriatric field and deny happiness to poor Stockard Channing. But now, without my love, I get it. Movie Christopher Plummer had the most amazing life with his chosen partner and it ended before he wanted it to. He's not looking for a replacement, because as far as he's concerned, there is no replacement for that. He's good. And he's confident enough to say that he's got what he needs. That sort of certainty isn't selfishness. It's power. God, I want that.

I can't say if I'm more a Sandra Bullock or a Christopher Plummer, because it's all too soon, and there aren't any hot handsome men offering me that choice yet. Right now it's just me and my empty bed and broken heart, and although there are parts of me—the lady parts—that occasionally remember that they like being used, the rest of me can't imagine ever opening myself up to this kind of hurt.

I hope I prove to be a combination of both characters, that I can square my loss and the end of the love I thought was forever. Even in this sad, damaged state, I can see how it would be nice to have love, or at least sex, again, because in the five years I was with Scott, I became quite fond of it, and I would really hate to think I had only a five-year sex window. But I also want to have enough faith in the love I had, to reconcile myself to the messy perfection of that, to know that even if I never find someone else, I got more happiness than a lot of people ever do.

But God, if You're reading this, know that I really, really hope that's not the case.

The thing about being a widow in the twenty-first century, as opposed to a hundred years ago, is that there is no socially accepted mourning period that governs when you can leave the house, how much unflattering black drapey shit you must wear and for how long, or when you get to date. Or whatever you want to call it.

Back in the day, they'd shame a widow for trying to get out there or marry too soon, unless the woman was culturally expected to marry her late husband's next-eldest unmarried brother or something. It's different now, but there are still rules. I've heard of couples who got together years after their respective spouses died but were still shunned by their circle, people who honestly needed to just thank Jesus for their still-breathing spouses and mind their damn business.

And look at how the tabloids and Twitter weigh in when a celebrity widow dares walk down the street with a person of the opposite sex—"Is she ready yet? Is it too soon?" Have a seat, Twitter. You don't get to decide this. The widows do. *I* do. I have no effing idea when I'll be ready. Maybe the answer will just fall on me from the sky. The universe loves dropping unexpected shit on me. Maybe I'll get hit with something nice this time.

Hearts are tricky and loneliness is a bitch, so the time frame for when I should even consider dating or whatever is shaky at best. I mean, you shouldn't bring a date to the funeral. Then again, grief is a gut punch, and I do not blame any widowed person for wanting to feel good, no matter what the feel-good thing is, because there is *so* much feeling bad.

One of the best things about being a couple, at least for me, is that having an automatic plus-one, a person who shows up. A designated hand-holder, an obligatory zipper-puller-upper when you can't reach all the way, a person who will kiss you—or do other stuff with you.

I miss other stuff.

Because of my waiting-for-marriage situation, I was finally hitting my stride in that department at about the time Scott died. When that happened, I immediately felt it all shut down, like, *Well, you did a good job, Leslie's sexuality. Thank you for your service these five years. You can go now.*

I didn't have any amorous feelings immediately after Scott died. I was too wrapped up in surviving, in raising my child and keeping him with me. Who has time for romantic thoughts when there's another social worker on her way to the house? But now, a few months later, I've started noticing things, like that I am a human woman. And that I am single. Then again, even imagining being with someone who's not Scott feels like being slapped in the face.

After having an anvil fall on your head. Right before the cement mixer drives over you. I'm basically Wile E. Coyote.

"When is this going to feel normal again?" I ask Sarah the therapist. Therapy must be working because talking to her about Scott no longer feels like picking off pieces of my skin with a pair of rusty pliers. One of the best things she has done for me is to get me to talk about being angry at him for dying.

"Because that was an awful thing for him to do," she says, and I laugh, because it's not only an absurd thing to say but also entirely true.

"It's okay to be mad at him for leaving you," she continues, and for a fleeting moment, I get really defensive and want to yell at her for implying that he did it on purpose, which of course he didn't. I sound this all out for Sarah, who nods. Then I take a deep breath and ask her how soon people want to date after being widowed. Not when they do date, just when they start to want to. I don't want to. Just curious.

"You mean, when you remember you're human?" she says.

Yeah, that.

Back when there were widow rules and black veils and such, you maybe didn't have to think of these things. Per the rules, one day when society decided you were ready, they just introduced you to the nice widower at church or the nice single butcher who sold Grandma the brisket. No one's brought me a nice butcher, so I'll have to fumble through this on my own when someone stumbles into view. Sure enough, soon after this conversation with Sarah, for the first time since Scott died, I find a man attractive.

Well, will you look at that!

It's true; I am out with friends and I notice a man. He's someone I already know, but I feel like I'm seeing him for the first time. I notice not just that he is cute, which is a start, but that he smiles. At *me*. And it feels nice. And he notices me and thinks I'm cute and tells me so.

Of course, since it's me, I put too much weight into what that smile might mean. I want to be wanted. I want to feel that thing that I chased for so long before I met Scott. But nothing happens with Smiling Man, even as we continue to hang out in groups. Smiling and telling me I'm cute? That was the whole movie, all thirty-seven seconds of it. Even if Smiling Man had made a move, I honestly wouldn't have known what to do with it. But I hold on to that little light that his smile switched on in me. And I hope that maybe when I'm ready, he'll like me too.

It would be nice if it led to something rom-com cute and

meaningful, but this, children, is not how the world works. It becomes apparent to me once I really am ready to date that this man is not going to date me. Smiling Man was not *my* man, and I'm embarrassed to say that it takes him introducing me to his girlfriend one day, in a very kind but public way, for me to accept that this is officially a non-starter. I am being, ever so gently, rejected.

Well, damn.

It's not really about this guy. It's that I am still in pain, that skin-flaying pain, and just thinking about him was soothing, like an ice cube.

"That's part of the healing," Sarah tells me, "knowing you can open yourself up to the possibility."

"When is that going to happen?"

She shrugs. "You'll know."

The Band-Aid is off now, and my heart's out there in the open, half healed, half hideous, and vulnerable to the elements.

After I've processed my embarrassment a little, I wonder what I'll do when it's time to actually try to date. I am not there yet, but I'm the kind of woman who does Zillow searches for real estate in every new city I go to, just in case I fall in love with it—research is my thing. I ask Sarah how one even goes about beginning to do this, and she suggests that when I even think that I might be ready, I should ask people I trust to fix me up.

It turns out that the older you get, the fewer non-asshole single people your friends know. You cannot fathom how many times I hear "I know the perfect guy for you, but he's married" or "He's perfect but he has a girlfriend" or "He's perfect but he's gay."

I know everyone is trying to help, but that's like offering me a selection of delicious cakes, telling me all about your favorite one, then adding, "But I made it just for Becky, so you can't eat it." Don't tell me about that cake. Leave the taken cakes out of the catalog. Only available cakes, please.

It still feels weird to think about other lips and other arms and other parts. I want the set that I married. I chose them for forever.

"You need a vibrator," a friend tells me. "Want me to buy you one?" She must immediately see the frozen, terrified look on my face, like I'm lost in Jurassic Park and just met my very first velociraptor, because she adds, "Tell me when you're ready." (That gift would come in the mail about a year later, and it would be a while before it made it out of the box. But it was wonderful to be looked out for in that way, to be understood and not judged and encouraged; as Sarah says, to be human.)

Sarah and my friends and even the suggested vibrator are nudging me onward, because I can't have the lips and arms and other parts I want back. Those, again, are lost to me.

Maybe kissing other lips will make me feel a little less lost. Eventually. When I'm ready.

About two years after Scott dies, at Camp Widow, I discover that some of the most popular workshops are about dating, attended by people who are ready to jump back into the game and those who just want to believe that they will be. There are no promises and they don't hand me a widowed hot person to hang out with along with my name tag and schedule.

What they give me is hope. Hope that someday, I will get proof that this part of me—the part that wants and is wanted—didn't die with Scott. I have more pressing things to deal with in the present, like keeping my kid and my job and not doing anything to make my mother want to flee to Cabo without a forwarding address.

But for now, it's enough that I want it. That feels all right to me.

16

The Once and Future Roommate

So how's it going with your mom?"

She and I have been living together now for about four months, and people are curious about the arrangement— a recently widowed mother and her more recently widowed daughter. It's a ready-made sitcom, meaning there are bound to be some fights, some growing pains, but then some single heart-to-hearts around the twenty-one-minute mark, before the closing credits kick in and we all hug and get to go to bed.

At first, we both try too hard to be polite—more polite than real mothers and daughters are to each other. Like, we're way too careful about not upsetting each other by leaving our purses in a place the other could trip over them or forgetting trash day or not buying the extra carton of almond milk like we promised. Everyone wants this to work out, and we don't want it to unravel because of something stupid like almond milk.

It is weird, though, living with her again. We're both grown women, with loss and lives and autonomy. But she's still Mommy, still my better. I am never going to be the kind of adult daughter who calls her mother by her first name or who thinks of herself completely as her mother's equal, because I'm not. She raised me, and the respect I have for her will always be in place. She's not one of my little friends, you know?

But I know that this new arrangement sometimes throws her off. There are times when I do stuff like forget to rinse out the sink and she goes back into yelling-at-thirteen-year-old-Leslie mode before she remembers that I'm not thirteen anymore. I'm not a child. I'm a grown woman, and she's living in what was my family home when my husband was alive. As much as I try to make her feel like this is *our* house, it's disconcerting for both of us.

Eventually we're probably going to have to move. Mommy and I need to start all over in a neutral space, and our dear little house, which was already too small for Scott, Brooks, me, and all our stuff, is just not going to cut it in the long-term with my mom and all her stuff there. Even with the expert pruning skills of Miss Johnnie, she's moved much of the contents of a big old house here, and the place is beginning to look like the inside of a clown car. Plus, it's only fair that we start over in a space that isn't mine or hers but ours.

Which means that we're headed into a new phase of commitment, with real estate agents and leases and two names on utility accounts. We are moving to a second location, and you know what they say about moving to a second location in an uncertain situation. Or maybe that's just about avoiding kidnappers?

"Are you sure you want to do this?" I ask my mother nervously, because I've been left before and would rather be prepared this time around.

"Of course. Are you?"

Yeah, I guess I am.

I keep thinking she wants to bounce, to finally put up a profile on OurTime.com, the official dating site for older people, so she can find a hot, rich widower and move to his private island. But she doesn't want to leave now, and I know that my constant spewing of guilt over derailing her plans for single widowhood is beginning to get on her nerves.

"Look," she says as I'm doing a tentative search through Realtor.com for smaller houses for rent, just in case, "I chose this. I chose you guys. I want to be here. Yes, I had a choice, and I'm choosing this."

In other words, *I'm trying to be reassuring but you're ruining it. Back off and let me love you.* The thing we have, besides love, is membership to the worst club ever—the widow club. That's one of the first things the two of us have in common that she doesn't also have in common with Lynne. I hope she never does. But that bond—that stupid, shitty bond—seems to make this weird transition from mother and daughter to roommates easier. There are times that I am sullen or angry or pissed at all the people in pharmaceutical commercials who didn't die of heart disease, and I'm less than reasonable. I lash out. I snap at her. I cry in the middle of a sentence, in the middle of a syllable.

And when my breath is normal again and the sobbing stops obscuring my speaking, I'll shake my head like a dog who just got washed and say, "I'm so sorry. I just miss my husband."

"I understand," my mother will say. And in those moments, I'm reminded that she really does.

We do have to move soon. Not only is the house too cramped, but I still feel Scott in every room. This was *our* house. We chose it together. I see him when I sit on the couch and look into the kitchen, imagine him making a sandwich or sitting in his Archie Bunker chair. I see him sitting on the edge of the bed playing Xbox in one of his jerseys. There he is, carefully navigating a massive load of dry cleaning down the narrow hall, the curve of the coat hangers scraping the paint on the wall as I yell, "I'm not repainting that when we get charged for it when we move!"

When Mommy and I do finally move, I know I'll feel like I'm leaving Scott behind. He and I had actually talked about moving someplace bigger together so Brooks could go to that excellent elementary school he'd read about. He wasn't even two years old yet, but Scott was already bringing home brochures for private school and sending me links about school rankings. He was way into this dad thing and well on his way to becoming one of those parents who say, "We can't send him to that low-rated second-grade class! He'll never get into Harvard." I'd mocked him thoroughly for this.

Undeterred by my mocking, Scott wanted Brooks in that excellent school, so it is now my mission to make that happen. During this time, I'm watching a lot of *House Hunters,* the HGTV program where couples, parents and children, and even single home buyers and nosy-ass friends visit three homes they're considering buying. Drama ensues, deal-breakers threaten, and the real estate agent is forced to say things like, "Well, Dana and Steve, I'm not sure if we're going to find a Federal townhome near the subway and your favorite bar with only gold carpet in the bathrooms that's been sprinkled with holy water blessed by Pope John Paul the Second in your price range. Might you consider a compromise?"

Of course, it's all staged and the couple's already picked a house. Non-fans love trying to burst your bubble with that knowledge, but I don't care. Can't I just look at the wainscoting and hardwood and Google what houses cost in Lawrence, Kansas? Stop ruining shit people like. What I like most about the show, besides the fact that you get to go on open-house visits without ever leaving your couch, is how much you can tell about someone's personality by the spaces he or she wants to be in. When my mom and I start looking for a new house—we're going to rent, at least initially—I pay attention to what she likes and doesn't like. I swear, you never get too old to be continually surprised that your parents are real people with tastes and preferences that have nothing to do with you.

Here is what I learn about my mother as we embark on

the house-hunting process: She likes a backyard. She'd prefer a garage, but a carport is fine. She likes houses with stairs, but as she gets older, she doesn't necessarily want to buy one. She likes a leather couch and a very giant TV. She was raised by people who lived through the Depression and doesn't waste food, so I've learned that if I can't find that broccoli that's been in the fridge for a week, it's because she froze it. (I don't remember her doing this when I was a kid. Maybe the four of us ate food too fast for it to be applicable.)

Soon enough, it turns out that all my hand-wringing and pondering whether or not we should move is moot. At the beginning of February, seven months after Scott died, our landlord calls to say that the house is on the market and since we're going month to month, he's letting us know that we have to be out in thirty days. The when-to-move decision is made for us. Thanks for the kick out the door, Fate!

We try not to panic and start the house search in earnest. The Zillow dress rehearsal is over and now it's showtime. There's suddenly nothing in our price range or preferred neighborhoods available. Also complicating the proceedings is that our moving deadline is right around what will be my first wedding anniversary without Scott, our sixth. I had planned to flee to Miami for a night with my friend Micah from Pennsylvania; she was going to let me drink and cry and stare at the ocean all I wanted. She has now offered to help me move instead, because she's good people.

As the days tick by, my mother and I see more houses than I can count, but nothing is right. Time is running out, and I know I have to suck it up and make a decision. We look at a house that's in a good neighborhood and close to both the water and the school that we want. However, it's old with no updates, a crappy kitchen, and no washer and dryer. "We can buy a washer and dryer," my mother whispers. We can live anywhere for a year, right? We shut up and fill out an application.

"So," I say to my real estate agent, pretty much as I'm handing him the pen back, "I don't suppose there's any chance..."

The eye roll is almost audible. "No," he says. "This is it. Nothing else is gonna open up in time."

That conversation is still fresh in my little Pollyanna brain when the phone rings early the very next morning. It's my real estate agent, telling me that a brand-new renovated single-family house on a corner of a very quiet street about two blocks from the Intracoastal Waterway just sprouted a For Rent sign in the front yard. He's already taken the liberty of calling the house's agent, and soon we have an appointment for that afternoon. I meet my mother there.

Before I'm out of the car, I'm already calculating the commute to my office and imagining my car in the driveway. I notice a few cars slowing down to take photos of the For Rent sign and I want to fling my body in front of it. *Nooo! You can't have it! My miracle! Mine! Shoo!*

My mom and I look at the place from the perimeter, silently. I'm almost scared to like it, scared that the thing I have wanted might be right here in front of me, ready to move into. Mommy notices another car rolling purposefully down the street, pausing for the driver to read the sign.

"It's the vultures coming for my house," I say. I haven't even seen the inside of it, but I'm already sticking a flag in this thing like a conquistador. I ain't playing.

And the minute the agent, whose name is Don, opens the door, I gasp. It's gorgeous.

"For real?" I whisper to Mommy.

I told you about how I've believed Jesus has specifically been sending crap my way for whatever reason. The second I saw this house I could feel Him gently poking me in the back and saying, *See, girl? I told you!*

It's got vaulted ceiling beams in the front room, with an expansive Florida room and a wall of sliding glass doors leading to the back patio. The backyard is full of trees and well-maintained shrubs. It also has a washing machine and dryer, so it's already better than the other place. They're in a separate building outside, but I don't have to buy them or put quarters in them, so it's cool.

There are three bedrooms, including the master, which I can only describe as an oversize privacy grotto. Don the agent explains that we are the first people to look at the place. He has a few other phone calls and appointments lined up, including a woman who's coming the next day.

I hope that woman finds a place, that her life is prosperous, and that her family does well. But not in my house.

Because this is my house.

And if they approve us, I'll be able to just write a check for the deposit, thanks to the life insurance, without having to mentally do the bank-account math in my head. So different from when you're young and broke and you're like, "Can I give you like half today and maybe, like, a fourth next Tuesday? And call me before you deposit that check, okay?"

Scott did his thing, y'all. He got us a house! And it was the house in the neighborhood with the good school, the one that he dreamed of Brooks attending. Scott will not be there to throw a ball with him or help him with his homework. But he did it.

I knew I was smart to marry that boy.

17

On with the Show

As we settle into our new place, my mother is hitting her stride with her new nursing teacher jobs, which means not only that there's more money in the house but also that she's fully committed to living here and really isn't going to up and leave me. That her mail comes here and that her name's on our lease next to mine should have been enough comfort for me. But this finally feels like the proof I need. You know how I am.

For the first time in a while, I let myself breathe. Everything is finally coming together and we know we're all gonna be happy forever with no uncertainty whatsoever.

Just kidding! It's spring now, about six months after the parental-rights hearing, and we made it through the appeals period without challenge from the birth parents. But that doesn't mean it's over. Ooh, boy, is it not over.

Remember the wishful thinking that we were possibly going to be done by the end of the year? Well, 2015 has ended, and 2016's almost half over, and we're still far from done. Now we have a different group of social workers, new people for me to send long and increasingly flustered e-mails to that might as well all have the subject line *What the hell is going on?*

What's going on is more paperwork and procedures. More waiting and more visits from the new social workers, although they've all been briefed and are really cool about the times when my toy-cluttered home is less than Donna Reed–esque. One very patiently fielded all my dumb questions about why our bathroom doorknob is not the approved kind and why we have to buy a new refrigerator thermometer. I understand the need for regulations. But the fixes aren't cheap.

I have more than one low moment when I get mad about the fact that it takes something really traumatic for the authorities to act on removing children from clearly hazardous situations in their original homes, and sometimes that removal doesn't happen until way too much damage has been done. No one's in there arbitrarily measuring the exact temperature of their refrigerators or making the parents run out to get a new thermometer to ensure it's dropped three degrees unless something bad has already happened. They're just in there, with the wrong doorknobs and not-quite-cold-enough fridges, while I'm jumping through all the hoops. Again, I get it. I signed up for this. It's just a list.

Along with our usual visits, we get home inspections from one of the ladies who taught our adoption classes and did the first home study with the good cheese before Brooks was even born. Seeing her lifts me, because she knew me back when I was half of Leslie and Scott. He wanted "Sceslie" for our mashup name. Even if he's not going to be on anything official—and I still hope he can be—at least there's someone involved who remembers how it was supposed to be. That doesn't matter legally, but it sure as hell matters to me. I remind our old social worker friend of Scott's frequent, passionate, and probably wrong answers in class, and she laughs.

"He was a wonderful man," she says, not mentioning if she remembers him threatening hypothetical racists with a baseball bat. "And he was, I'm sure, an amazing father. I'm so sorry he won't be here to make it official."

I am too, but I haven't yet given up on him having some official connection. I have been asking, more and more emphatically as the months go by, whether or not it's possible to have Scott's name on the birth certificate. I don't love the idea of the updated birth certificate in the first place. After all, I wasn't the one in that hospital giving birth to him. Brooks's biological parents shouldn't be written out of his official history. I think the policy is a relic from back when adoptions were closed and some parents lied to their kids about it. But whether I like it or not, once the adoption is final, a new birth certificate will be issued, and there's no place to note that the parents are adoptive. I have a copy of Brooks's original birth certificate, and I'm always going to be open with him about where he came from and who his biological parents are.

Since Brooks is getting a new birth certificate, I want Scott to be on it. I couldn't keep him alive. I couldn't stop his heart attack, couldn't save him when he was dying right in front of me. The least I can do is get his name written on a damn piece of paper. If I can't, I'll feel like I've failed him yet again. You don't think you can disappoint a dead guy. But you can.

"Please," I say to our wonderful Maryland social worker. "Anything you can do." She tells me she'll do her best. She knows it's going to break me all over again if she can't make it happen.

At least I've made a decision about Brooks's last name, and it's a hard one. Scott did not want it hyphenated; he wanted Brooks to be a Zervitz, full stop. I am always going to be Leslie Gray Streeter professionally, but I had agreed to finally legally change my last name to Zervitz once the adoption was done so we could all have the same last name. It wasn't a priority before the baby and, honestly, I don't think Scott cared that much about my name; this was about Brooks. Scott needed to be able to say they were both in this together, from the heart to the name. They belonged to each other.

Now, with Scott gone, it seems morbid to legally change my last name to Zervitz because we are not actively married to each other anymore, the "M" being replaced with a "W" on official forms, and, yes, it feels as shitty as it sounds. Still, as a widowed single mother, I want to have the same last name as my child; it's emotional, practical, and political. A lot of people assume that single mothers of color are somehow less than, that there's something morally wrong with us, and that we're out here having all these kids we don't share our last names with because we don't know the fathers' names or something like that. I shouldn't care what those people think. Screw those people. I don't owe racists and judge-y assholes a damn thing. And if I had never been married, that wouldn't be anyone's business.

But sharing some portion of a name with Brooks does make it easier to get on a plane with him or register him for school or Little League. I've heard from dads who are married to or with the mothers of their kids but who have different last names than them that it's sometimes a hassle. For all these reasons, part of me thinks it makes the most sense for Brooks's last name to be Streeter. But I just can't cut Scott out of it. So even though Scott was always against hyphenating, I decide that Brooks will be Brooks Robinson Streeter-Zervitz, and I'm going to remain Leslie Gray Streeter, the Zervitz existing just in my heart.

Brooks, at least, will have both our names in there somewhere. Sorry, Scotty. It's not what it's supposed to be, but then, what the hell is?

After we get the name all sorted out, we still have two important adoption-related in-person visits coming up soon. The first will be the social worker who did the classes with Scott and me, the other our longtime adoption worker from Baltimore, who is doing a final home inspection. I like her a lot, but her visit presents yet another opportunity for me to freak out and assume that everything is going to fall apart.

What if she gets all the way down here and there's something off about the house, something that makes her question every decision she and the court have made in our favor for the past almost three years? We're doing so well and she's going to see that. Brooks seems good. He loves our new house and its backyard full of trees, mysterious corners, and space aplenty for him to dig holes with his toy excavator and bulldozer. He tells us these are his "struction sites," and we don't correct him. He's trying to do a thing, and what's more, he's got imaginary roadwork to do. There are photos of Scott everywhere and sometimes I see Brooks pause on the way to create some beautiful mess and noise and just look.

"I miss him too," I say, and that seems to be enough for the moment.

While he's loving the new place, he still hasn't forgotten the one we lived in before; he points out the intersection every time we drive by. "That's where our old house was," he says, and my heart feels deeply itchy because that's the last place he saw Scott. I don't think until we've really settled into the new house that it becomes plain just how much I needed to move, how much pain and memory I had been holding there physically, how impossible it had been for me to move on before we actually moved.

But I'm not the only one needing to move on. I've been going back to our street, past that old house, to take walks with my former neighbor Liz. Every time I see it, I'm a little less sad, a little less haunted. One morning I decide to pack Brooks and the running stroller in the car with me to go meet her, and as we drive around the roundabout at our old corner on the way to her house, I hear a little voice from the back seat.

"That's the old house, where Daddy is," he says.

Oh, man. Did we not have this conversation already?

Brooks doesn't seem mad or sad, but his little brain is still working this out. It hasn't been quite a year, but I don't know what any of that means to him. And now, on this early-morning drive, I realize he hasn't quite understood the permanence. I feel so shitty and guilty, and I know I can't be vague about this one more minute.

"Sweetie," I say, pulling over in front of Liz's house and turning around so Brooks can see me, "Daddy's not in that house. Daddy's"—*Oh, Leslie, just say it*—"Daddy died. He died and he's in Heaven and he's not coming back. I'm so sorry."

God. This hurts. But not like I thought. It's always going to be awful to say what I'm saying, but the need to do it, now, both numbs me and gives me a little more guts.

I turn off the car, reach back, and take Brooks's little hand, and his eyes widen slightly, because we're getting super-serious at six a.m. "Baby," I say, trying again, "if Daddy was still alive, if he could be with us, there's no way that he'd be in this house down here without us. You'd have to fight that man to keep him away from you, away from us. He's not here, and we can't see him, but he's with us. Does that make sense?"

My son looks at me, eyes still wide, and I don't know what he's feeling, because he still doesn't have the language to break it down, therapy-style. And he can't absolve me of any damage I might have done by not explaining it in a way that didn't make him believe his father was hanging out a mile away. But this moment isn't about me, so I push through it.

"Okay," he says, nodding, and he looks out the window and points out Liz and her dog on the sidewalk. And just like that, I've done it. I don't yet know what "Okay" means, but it's going to have to do.

When the social worker from Maryland arrives for our last visit, this and so many other things are on my mind, and I've been pacing in the kitchen all morning. She's as warm as I remember, and she's immediately charmed by Brooks's smile. She is, in that way that good social workers are, confident and reassuring without making promises. The important thing here is that she tells me, pretty much as soon as she walks in, that it's going to happen.

"It's gonna happen?"

"It's gonna happen."

Oh my God. It's real. The tears come so fast I can barely see. The moment is a glorious exclamation point, but in my worry-prone mind, it's attached to an invisible asterisk.

Of course, "gonna happen" doesn't yet have a date, but it's sure enough that the social worker is opening her calendar and showing me available days for the finalization, when Brooks will finally be mine, legally, for real.

"How about July twenty-second?" she says. The thunderbolts come clapping around my ears, because even math-challenged me realizes that's very near another date in July, a date that looms so ominously that it feels like a Macy's Thanksgiving Day parade balloon losing air above my face.

"That's the week before the anniversary of Scott's death," I say. Oh, how I hate saying those words. "Like, exactly a week."

She nods. "That might be nice, to have something positive around that date to always remember, right?"

I nod back. The end of July is going to suck for the rest

of my life. But it'll now be home to one of the best anniversaries of my life, right before the absolute worst. I finally feel like God has done me a solid.

While I'm silently thanking the heavens, she starts to say something, then pauses. And I just know that this is our asterisk. Here's the *but.*

"So, the birth certificate," she says, and all of the *Yay!* in the world can't change what's coming, which is that no matter how much Scott is Brooks's father in my heart, no matter how much he was and continues to be, he will not be his official father in the eyes of the State of Maryland, because the birth certificate and adoption decree are legal documents that someone has to sign. And Scott is not here to do that.

Oh no.

"Are you sure?" I say, my voice too high and my eyes too wild. I am not the first distraught person the social worker has just dropped bad news on, so she's prepared for the fallout. She squeezes my hand, and it's funny to realize that for nearly three years, she's been one of the most important people in my life. I don't really know anything about her, which I guess is how it's supposed to be. But I do know that she's breaking my heart even as she's saving my life.

"He is his father. He is. Scott is his father," she says. "And

I am so sorry that we aren't going to be able to do this for you, but he is going to have Scott's name. It's a beautiful name. And everyone will know that Scott was his father. That's all that counts."

I don't really agree, but I get it. She's done all she can. It's not enough, but it is what it is. It's a victory. Brooks is, very soon, going to legally be my boy.

That alone is worth a parade.

18

You're Gonna Make
It After All

The couple of months between the social worker's visit and the adoption finalization date at the end of July fly by. Brooks is still thriving in day care, and I'm trying to explain to him what's about to happen. It's a big deal, and I want him to know it.

"You know how those ladies always come by the house to visit you and ask you questions? They aren't going to be doing that anymore, because we're gonna dress up and go sit with a judge and she's going to say that you are now officially, all the way, Mommy's boy! And we're gonna have a party with everyone who loves us, and there'll be cake!"

Brooks has already learned the important skill of tuning one's mother out, but now he looks up. "Cake?" he says, brightening. "I like cake!"

Honestly, that's the most I can expect from a not-yet-three-year-old. I'm going to have to be excited enough for both of us. In a few years, we'll show him the pictures and he'll get it then.

Right now, all we have left to do is a tiny bit more paperwork and the formal hearing with the judge. This time, though, there won't be any lawyers or testimony or any possibility of messing this up. It's just a formality, a beautiful, public one. And there will be parties and, yes, cake. More than one cake. In two different states. Both are going to be fun and full of people who have loved Brooks and me through this year. God, what a year.

But first, we have to get this boy officially adopted. I buy Brooks a suit and a jaunty hat for the occasion. For myself, I find a purple dress—Ravens colors for Scotty!—that looks like what your mom might wear to your wedding or what an overdressed municipal employee might wear to her boss's goodbye party where everyone else is dressed like *Aren't we just having punch and cake by the copier?*

It's probably too much, but this is going to be a Happening, so I'm going to dress that way. I want it all. I want the gavel. I want the long, slow walk through official-looking judge's chambers. I want to cry and hug and have really awesome photos taken. I've climbed out of hell by the tips of my raggedy fingernails. A Happening is the least I deserve.

The plan is to leave West Palm for Baltimore really early the day before the big ceremony so we can get settled in and be well rested for the next day.

Plans are cute.

Perhaps because I'm super-jazzed and focused on our trip, it doesn't seem weird to me the day before the flight that my mother can't log into Southwest's website to check in.

"That's odd," she says. "But we'll just get to the airport extra-early tomorrow."

We are not a timely family, so I count it as a major victory when we're easing into the Uber around four thirty a.m. with plenty of time to make our flight. I can feel my phone ringing in my pocket. Hey, it's Southwest Airlines. What a coincidence! We're just on our way to fly on one of their fine airplanes! I scramble to get the phone to my ear and hear a recorded lady say that she is really sorry but our flight has been canceled.

Huh.

Recorded Lady suggests calling Southwest to make further arrangements. I feel acid beginning to form in my mouth and slide down my chest, but I shake it off. No. This is just a glitch. Southwest must have a whole day's worth of flights to get us there. If something bad's happening with this one, we'll find another. I start calling the airline while we're making our way to the airport, trying to talk to a human being.

It's going to be okay.

I am still on hold fifteen minutes later as the Uber drops us off at Palm Beach International Airport, where we immediately notice a longer-than-usual line streaming from the Southwest ticket desk at this early hour. We ask a random lady what's going on, and she tells us that her flight was canceled the night before and that she was told to come back to try to get on the flight we were on.

Supposed to be on.

Everyone around us has similar stories of canceled flights. No one knows exactly what is going on. I am trying not to freak out, but it's not working too well. As we go nowhere in the line that never ends, I am still on hold with the airline, and the cute little hold messages featur ing folksy Southwest employees are beginning to make me furious.

We look to the front of the line and try to read the faces of the people that have already gotten to speak to an agent. Do they look happy? Relieved? Angry? About to start breaking stuff?

"What did they say?" we ask a guy walking away from the counter. He tells us that Recorded Phone Message Lady was right—our flight, the first one scheduled to Baltimore this morning, is canceled, as is the next one. And the one after that is all full of the people who were supposed to be on those two flights and the one the night before.

"Oh no, oh no, oh no," I start to chant, apparently not as under my breath as I think. I am going to that dark place, and every bit of Pollyanna is being pushed out of my gut to make way for Marion Crane from *Psycho*. She's naked and dripping in a shower in a mouth-open death mask as Norman Bates's knife appears above her and she knows she's screwed.

I feel a hand on my arm.

"No," my mother says. "We're not doing this. You are not going to freak out right now."

"I'm not? I'm pretty sure I am."

"No, you are not," Mommy insists. "You are going to calm down and wait to get some facts and not make it worse by borrowing trouble you don't have yet."

"I heard someone talking about Russian hackers! That's trouble! Look at all these people!"

My mother leans over, smile gone, and looks me in the eye. Uh-oh. She is a calm person usually, but when she looks at you like this, you might be in trouble.

"Do you believe that this adoption is in our plan?"

"Yes."

"Then it's going to happen." If she were Bette Davis in an old movie or a Real Housewife, she might have slapped me across the face to snap me out of it or at least thrown a table over. But Tina Streeter is classier than that. Thank you, Mommy, for not being a Real Housewife.

When we finally get to the counter, I'm a little calmer, which is to say I'm no longer rocking back and forth and chanting anymore. The agent tells us what we already know, which is *we're screwed!*

Okay, that's not what he says, but it feels like it. There was some massive outage with the Southwest system the night before, and all of Southwest's flights everywhere were grounded. This morning, planes are supposed to be flying, but as you might imagine, the airline has had to scramble to un-strand all the people from last night. Basically, we're going to be fighting a lot of people for seats. We've established that I am willing to fight. I will fight folks.

"Is there any way that you can fly tomorrow?" the agent says.

"No, we can't," I say. "My son's adoption is happening first thing tomorrow morning in Baltimore and we have got to get there sometime today."

I am personally familiar with the rampant lies told to customer service people, having been lied to professionally myself, all the sob stories about how someone's grandma died or how the family farm is about to be sold or how some guy's sister's been tied to the railroad tracks and he needs to get there with the deed to the ranch *right now* to save her. When I worked at a movie-theater concession stand, people would make up sob stories to cut ahead in the popcorn line so they wouldn't have to miss a minute of *Batman*. It makes sense that the customer service people don't believe anybody.

So I'm prepared to have to convince this man that I'm telling the truth. I am actually about to reach into my bag to get the papers with the date and time of the adoption ceremony when he smiles.

"I want to help you," he says. "You have to get there." My faith in humanity is temporarily restored.

The agent is clicking away on the computer. I'm starting to feel hopeful, when...

"Nope."

Nope?

"Maybe this." *Click-click-click.* "No."

I don't like "No." Is it illegal to bribe Southwest ticket agents? Ha, ha, ha, joking, Government!

"Wait," the agent says, saving me from ever having to find out. "We have the eight-thirty tonight out of Fort Lauderdale. Do you think you could make it there?"

"Done," I say. "Yes, please. Get us on that."

Click, click, click and we're confirmed. The nice agent warns us that there are a lot of people trying to get out, obviously, and that more flights could be canceled, so we should get down to Lauderdale, about forty-five minutes away, good and early.

"Got it," I say, and I call another Uber to take us back home. This is gonna work out! God doesn't hate me! Probably!

I spend the day at our house in a panic, calling Southwest every half hour to make sure that our new flight hasn't been canceled. I trust no one at this point. Brooks, who loves planes and is disappointed he's not yet on one, refuses to nap for fear he's going to miss the flight. He knows there's something going on, and he seems to have decided it's a conspiracy to keep him off this plane. You can't fool him. He's almost three!

"No nap!" he insists. "Getting on the airplane!"

"I promise," I say as I sling him over my shoulder and toss him into his room, "that we are absolutely not trying to miss this particular airplane."

Several hours later, as we're in our third Uber of the day, this time to Fort Lauderdale, I look over at Brooks and wonder how much of my nervousness over the past year he might have picked up on. How much of my sadness, my anger. The times I curled up in the bathroom and sobbed and hoped he didn't hear me because I needed at least one of us to believe that everything was all going to be okay. When we went to the pediatrician the morning of the funeral, the doctor told me that if I was healthy, he would be too. Am I? Is he?

"I'm doing everything right, right?" I say to my mother. "I'm a good mom, right?"

"Yes, little girl," she says, kissing me on the forehead. "You're doing everything right."

"Everything" is a stretch. Nobody does everything right. But as we whiz down I-95 to the airport to the airplane that will take us to the end of this part of this soap opera, I can't help but wonder...

...I know I'm far gone now. I've resorted to Carrie Bradshaw ellipses.

Have I been so focused on the goal that I missed something, did something that might mess Brooks up? I want to be the best for him. Scott and I together would have been better. But this version of the best is all I can shoot for now.

"Two states have agreed that you are the best for him, and you can't get state governments to agree on anything," Mommy says. That's probably true.

Once at the airport, we jump out of the car and start to hustle. This airport is a lot bigger than Palm Beach International. When we finally get to our gate, I see that it is scarily crowded. Everybody looks super-tired and pissed off, so I know we're in the right place. We're not leaving for a while so we go to the nearby Tex-Mex restaurant in the terminal and I inhale a whole guacamole appetizer by myself and wash it down with a ginormous fruity spring-break-esque margarita. This won't get us in the air any sooner. But salt and tequila are remarkably soothing.

When an announcement comes on, you can feel the collective holding of breath. The announcement is that they have canceled the Baltimore flight right before ours. This ain't good. There's a roar building, and the clanging of bags and feet as people rush toward the gate to plead their cases as to why they should bump someone else.

We're told that our flight, the very last one for tonight,

will be taking off late but at least taking off, as soon as they find enough crew members. You'd think that after all this delay, there would be crew members hiding behind a coffee cart somewhere ready to go, because they've got to be as sick of this as we are.

We are, at least, assured that as long as this flight leaves, we have confirmed seats on it. I go back over to the table where my stuff is, and now there's a worried-looking family next to us. They're tired and fried and just want to go home. Their daughter, who I learn is a junior at a Pennsylvania college about two hours away from the airport in Baltimore, is getting particularly agitated.

"I'm going to my friend's twenty-first birthday party. I really need to get there," she says. "She's my *best* friend." I see her looking around and obviously playing the same game in her head I was playing before our seats were confirmed, which we'll call "Who Will Voluntarily Give Me His or Her Seat on This Plane?" On less important flights, if it's announced that they're offering money or a free travel voucher if you give up your seat, I've happily agreed and started planning my next fun trip courtesy of Whoever Airlines. That day is not today.

This girl is on the flight we are on, so they should be okay, but she seems afraid of getting bumped. She's looking for allies, and maybe she smells the margarita on me, but she seems to sense a connection. Normally, I would understand the need for this twenty-one-year-old to celebrate with her friend. "I *reallllly* want to go," she says again, opening her big earnest doe eyes wide. "It's really important."

This is some impressive *Les Mis* consumptive-waif-dying-on-the-street-corner shit, and I know she wants me to say that if there's a scramble, I'll give her my seat so she can go drink with her friends. I applaud her effort. But it's not going to happen.

"Well," I say, "my husband died last year before we could finalize our son's adoption, and tomorrow at nine a.m. we have to be there at the courthouse, and if we do not get on this plane, we are going to miss his adoption."

Shameless? Certainly. But effective. Daughter looks at me, stunned, because even in her desperation, she knows she's been bested. She never had a chance.

Her father leans over to her, pats her sympathetically on the shoulder. "She wins," he tells her, gesturing to me.

Why, yes! Yes, I do!

Around ten thirty p.m., they find the elusive crew member and they ask us to start lining up. Once we're sunk into our seats, I feel my lungs expand. I am breathing. We are going. This is happening.

By the time we land, it's after midnight, and we make our way to the rental-car facility and then eventually to the hotel that my aunt Reverend Debbie has thoughtfully booked us. I pass out with my son who will, tomorrow, officially be my son on paper. Paper means nothing. And yet it means everything.

We manage to sleep for about four hours, which is not enough but is going to have to be. I pull myself together in this dress I'm not sure I love anymore but will have to feel fabulous in because there's no time for feeling anything less than fabulous. I put the man of the hour in his suit and shake my mom awake. She looks wonderful, as expected, and we load ourselves into the rental to get all the way across I-695. Which, of course, is a parking lot.

"*Goooooo!*" I scream at all the other cars. "*Gooooo! You have to go!*"

"That's not working," my mother says. She is way observant.

I'm hoping that we're going to get there before someone calls to see where we are, because until that happens, we can play it off like we're not late and there's no need to panic. Of course, that's when the phone rings.

"Miss Streeter," our Maryland social worker says, and for the first time in a long time, I hear worry in her voice.

Not you too! Somebody has to be holding it together. She explains that there is another adoption scheduled after us, so if we're running late, they'll let the other family go before us. Crisis averted. As long as these damn cars get out of my way.

But they do, and when we finally get to the courthouse, we move through security faster than I thought, then stand restlessly in the elevator for what seems like a thousand hours, waiting for the doors to open. And holy crap, there's everyone I know standing there in the hallway. I feel like dead Kate Winslet at the end of *Titanic,* when she's young again and walks into the not-sunk grand hall of the ship and is greeted by all the other dead people, including young Leonardo DiCaprio. Everyone who needs to be here is here.

Except one person, of course.

In the corner, I see faces I haven't seen in more than a year. There's Brooks's former foster family and their new baby. Everything I have been holding on to breaks as we reach for one another. They look at Brooks, who used to have a different name but is the same baby they loved, and we all sob. It is sweet and bittersweet, and it feels just right. The circle is not unbroken. It is strong and wide and winds through some unbelievably thick and crazy places. But it comes together, full and solid, at the end. It's a circle, after all.

My brother-in-law Josh is here, and he ties Brooks's tie correctly because apparently I did it wrong, and it reminds me that Josh is here as Scott's representative. At least I know Brooks has one person in his life who can tie a tie. Brooks's attorney as well as all of the social workers who have helped us are here, and there are so many hugs and kisses that I'm drowning in them. I am breathing love through my nostrils.

It's time now for us to head back to the judge's chambers. We sit in front of her desk, my mom and I, the toddler in the hat on my lap holding my hand. The judge welcomes all of us and says that there will be plenty of time for photos later. And then it starts.

"We are here in the matter of the petition of Leslie Gray Streeter," she begins, and the name unsaid rings in my ears. There is no *and Scott Mitchell Zervitz*.

No, my heart wails. *This is not right. You are supposed to be here. This is supposed to be us. Just you and me and our boy. Why aren't you here?*

I am here. Shut up and listen, Scott whispers to me so clearly I can feel his stubble in the tender part of my ear. *Let her speak.*

"It is my pleasure to order, this twenty-second day of July 2016, by the Circuit Court of Baltimore County, that the male minor mentioned in these proceedings is hereby declared to be the legally adopted child of Leslie Gray Streeter."

And Scott Mitchell Zervitz, my heart repeats. *And Scotty. Scott's his daddy.*

Of course I am, Scott says, though only I can hear. *Stop talking. You're missing it.*

I don't notice that I am sobbing because I'm busy talking to my dead husband, but the judge does. She smiles and continues.

"It is further ordered that the name of said adoptee is hereby changed to Brooks Robinson Streeter-Zervitz."

It always was, Scott says.

It always was, I agree.

And then we're rushed, like celebrities, by all these people—friends and relatives and county workers and everyone who has been our family, who has helped this happen and kept me off a zillion ledges. They are all here to hug and love us.

Except Scott.

I am here! he yells, because I just won't stop. And that's okay. I never do.

I carry my new son, who was always my son, out of the courtroom, and we pose for many photos. Then we head to the Jewish deli we always used to go to with Scott so his aunts can buy us kugel and say mazel tov and comment on what a good boy Brooks is. They tell me that they know Scott would be so proud.

"I hope so," I blubber. "I hope he would be proud."

Someone orders some wine, and I raise my glass.

"To Brooks," I say. "And to Scotty Z."

L'chaim, Scott says in my ear. *But don't stay too long. This isn't the end of anything. It's just the beginning.*

Normally, I hate when other people have the last word. But just this once, I suppose it's okay.

About the Author

Leslie Gray Streeter is an entertainment columnist for the *Palm Beach Post*. Her writing has been featured in the *Miami Herald, Modern Loss,* and elsewhere. Streeter's many speaking engagements include annual appearances at Camp Widow, a program of Soaring Spirits International, an organization for widowed men and women that reaches nearly five hundred thousand people, and a series of book-club events for women. She lives in West Palm Beach, Florida, with her mother, Tina, and son, Brooks.